UKRAINIAN PORTRAITS

PORTRAITS

Diaries from the Border

ESSENTIAL PROSE SERIES 214

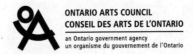

Guernica Editions Inc. acknowledges the support of
the Canada Council for the Arts and the Ontario Arts Council.
The Ontario Arts Council is an agency of the Government of Ontario.

We acknowledge the financial support of the Government of Canada.

MARINA SONKINA

UKRAINIAN PORTRAITS

Diaries from the Border

GUERNICA
EDITIONS

TORONTO · CHICAGO · BUFFALO · LANCASTER (U.K.)
2023

Guernica Founder: Antonio D'Alfonso

Michael Mirolla, editor
Interior and cover design: Rafael Chimicatti
Front cover image: Włodzimierz Milewski
Guernica Editions Inc.
287 Templemead Drive, Hamilton, ON L8W 2W4
2250 Military Road, Tonawanda, N.Y. 14150-6000 U.S.A.
www.guernicaeditions.com

Distributors:
Independent Publishers Group (IPG)
600 North Pulaski Road, Chicago IL 60624
University of Toronto Press Distribution (UTP)
5201 Dufferin Street, Toronto (ON), Canada M3H 5T8

First edition.
Printed in Canada.

Legal Deposit—Third Quarter
Library of Congress Catalog Card Number: 2023934993
Library and Archives Canada Cataloguing in Publication
Title: Ukrainian portraits : diaries from the border / Marina Sonkina.
Names: Sonkina, Marina, 1952- author.
Series: Essential prose series ; 214.
Description: 1st edition. | Series statement: Essential prose series ; 214
Identifiers: Canadiana (print) 20230200591 | Canadiana (ebook) 2023020080X
| ISBN 9781771838542 (softcover) | ISBN 9781771838559 (EPUB)
Subjects: LCSH: Sonkina, Marina, 1952- —Travel—Ukraine. | LCSH: Ukraine—
History—Russian Invasion, 2022- | LCSH: Ukraine—History—Russian
Invasion, 2022- —Personal narratives. | LCSH: Ukraine— Social conditions—
21st century. | LCSH: Women, Ukrainian—Social conditions—20th century. |
LCSH: Ukrainians—Social conditions—20th century.
LCGFT: Personal narratives. | LCGFT: Creative nonfiction.
Classification: LCC DK508.852 .S66 2023 | DDC 947.7086—dc23

CONTENTS

I dedicate these stories to heroic Ukrainian people who—I firmly believe—will prevail over the forces of Evil.

1. At the Border

ON FEBRUARY 24, 2022, Putin attacked Ukraine, launching the largest and the most brutal war on the European continent since WWII. Very quickly, in Russia, expressing any negative sentiments towards what was officially called a "special operation", would become a criminal offence. But then, in the early days of the invasion, an anonymous Russian woman bared her feelings in a post on the internet: "Overnight it became totally irrelevant how one looks; what kind of clothing one wears, what kind of films one watches. There is no point in any entertainment; no point in creative work or anything else. Food has no taste. Everything that has been familiar has totally lost its meaning."

Her emotions mirrored mine: bewilderment, numbness, stupor, inability to work, to focus on anything unrelated to the war, unfolding half a globe away from me, that' s what I felt in these early days of invasion. Why? What for? No amount of political buzz could provide answers to these vexing questions.

I was born and raised in Moscow and spent there half of my professional life. My two sons were born there. I still have family both in Russia and Ukraine. For many years, I've been teaching Russian literature and the classical questions the classical Russian writers always asked "who is to blame" or "what is to be done?" could never be more poignant than at this pivotal moment of history.

Clearly, the war with Ukraine was unleashed by Putin. But was he the only culprit? Haven't Russians been turning a blind eye to the twenty-three years of his rule while he was poisoning and executing his opponents? Didn't they welcome the annexation of Crimea while taking a stroll along the theatrical sets that Moscow has been turned into? Or was there some invisible point of no return when a burgeoning democracy turned into autocracy, then into fascism? When any attempts at resistance – and there were many – would be doomed? Did the West play any role in it, looking at Putin as at a business partner first, an authoritarian second? And what would be the fate of Ukraine, the fate of Russia and Europe in the years to come?

History seemed to be exposing its nuts and bolts. But it wasn't providing any answers or telling me which turn it would take next.

In this state of confusion, I decided to help Ukrainian refugees. My friends responded readily and generously to the fundraising I organized. My goal was to give this money directly to refugees, from hand to hand. But how to go about it, I didn't know. Things started to gain steam when I saw on my computer screen an application form from the JDC (Jewish Distribution Committee). I quickly filled it out and was interviewed next day. By that time close to two million refugees had already crossed the border into Poland. Volunteers and interpreters were urgently needed. I had to arrive in Warsaw the following Monday. It was already Friday. I had a week-end to fill out numerous forms and then pack.

It was the end of March.

2

The flight from Vancouver, Canada to Europe takes a day. Around midnight, I arrived in Warsaw. Derek, a Pole, who had been working for JDC tirelessly, on three-four hours of sleep, asked me if I wanted to see right then what it was all about or should he take me to the hotel for some rest? He put my suitcase into his van and five hours later I and two other volunteers from the US arrived to the Ukrainian-Polish border.

With no booths or guards in sight, it didn't look to me like a border. It was dark, windy and bitterly cold. The atmosphere was sombre; asking questions somehow didn't feel right. I decided we were taken to a special crossing, designated for some special purpose. There was nothing around, except a German Red Cross ambulance brightly illuminated from inside. Next to it, on the ground, were placed seven stretchers. Their white fabric contrasted sharply with the night darkness upon dark gravel. It was the sight of these stretchers, empty for now but soon to be filled with sick or wounded, that shocked me into the realization that the war zone was at hand.

Half an hour later, a bus from Ukraine with Holocaust survivors had arrived. As I found out later, Germany had made special arrangements to take them in. Six or seven frail women in their late eighties and nineties and one man

11

were helped out of the bus. They clung to their old-fashioned, worn out purses and plastic bags, all they had by way of luggage. The man, as far as I could tell, didn't have anything at all in his hands. Most of the women could walk if helped. But one, extremely emaciated, was unconscious, either wounded or sick. The German nurses (all volunteers) administered intravenous. From their conversation I understood they weren't sure the lady would make it to Germany. One woman seemed terribly distraught: nervously turning her handbag inside out, she refused to go any further. A watch, her late husband's present, was missing. Finally, she settled on a stretcher, her handbag on top of her chest. Some women didn't realize there was another long journey to endure. They had been on the road for 15 hours already crossing Ukraine. As far as they were concerned, they had already arrived. The man sitting at the back of the bus looked unperturbed: "I've started my life with one war. And now I'm finishing it with another. Does it matter to me where to die?"

In the next three weeks, I met hundreds more victims of Putin's war. Listening to them I realized that the war had laid bare what was usually concealed from the eyes of a stranger: human attachments and loves, support for one another and acts of kindness. But also, the seismic faults running through so many families; their discontents, their arguments, and the way they deal with them in the time of crises.

Inadvertently, I became privy to the lives of many simply because I happened to be there at the time of their great vulnerability and need. Those I met (and, with rare exceptions, these were women with children) were traumatized. All needed practical help, advice, information and, above all, empathy.

But what they also needed, I discovered, was to talk about what they had gone through. That need was spontaneous and raw. They broke into stories often without any or just a slight invitation on my part. Each story was different, yet many followed a similar pattern: destruction and loss of property or homes; weeks in basements with scarcely any water, food supplies and electricity; the howl of air raid sirens; separation from loved ones and concern about their well-being; screams of traumatized children; and, then, finally escape, over many days. Escape on foot, by trains, buses or sometimes cars, with detours necessitated by rockets and missiles; crossing rivers on boats where bridges were blown up.

I heard repeated gratitude towards Ukrainian volunteers who facilitated the escapes, relaying families from one safe place to another; warning about the dangers on the way and how to bypass them. I heard stories of churches that sheltered families overnight; of people harbouring strangers in their homes; of volunteers who organized food that awaited fleeing families at different points of their long and hazardous journey to safety. I learned a new word – *humanitarka*, meaning clothing, food and other necessities that poured into Ukraine from the West as humanitarian aid.

And I heard stories of the brutality of Russian soldiers towards civilians. Stories of looting, torture and rape. I heard how Russian soldiers pretended they would allow villagers to run to safety, only to shoot them in their legs, and finish them off later like hunted animals.

I heard stories of booby-trapped corpses, of Russians abandoning their dead. Of little girls being raped in view of their parents.

In the weeks I volunteered with the JDC at a border crossing and in a temporary refugee shelter several kilometres away from the border with Ukraine, I met people of all walks of life. I met the Ukrainian Nation.

I met a grandmother who escaped missiles with her six grandchildren and made it to Poland while the parents of the children had perished.

I met a welder, looking after his old, infirm and incontinent mother. They couldn't possibly inconvenience any family, the man explained, because he needed to clean up after her. The welder was now trying to bring to Poland his former wife with her new husband and their three children, one of whom was his.

I met sixty elderly Baptists from Zaporizhzhia on the way to Amsterdam, where a sister Baptist church was going to shelter them. Zaporizhzhia is the site of the largest atomic plant in Europe overtaken by Russian troops in the first days of war and then in October seized by Russia all together. It's the city where my relatives live in the region annexed by Russians as a result of sham referenda.

I discovered that the most painful subject that came up in conversations was the fact that women had had to leave their loved ones behind. The worry for their soldier sons and husbands, their parents, grandparents and siblings, was a deeply hidden, yet constant, heartbreak. A breaking point for many.

When a collective image of Ukraine comes to my mind, it's women's eyes. I will not forget those eyes, dozens and dozens of women's eyes: blue, grey, greenish; eyes magnified by tears at the thought of their loved ones left behind. Embarrassed to cry in front of me, a stranger, they tried to look away. The older sister would often say to the younger: "Enough already, just stop it!" while breaking into tears herself.

Another move that caused tears was the money. In Canada, I had packed lots of envelopes for a civilized handout. How naïve I was! In the chaos of a refugee transition centre, it was quickly handing over bills from hand to hand. A scared look and the initial refusal to accept was universal. I had to come up with some strategy to overcome the mutual embarrassment. "This is from Canadians. From my friends; friends of my friends. They want to help you. But they can't be here. They asked me to do it for them. Please take it."

A grateful look. Tears. A hug.

The Korzcowa refugee centre was a temporary shelter. Refugees could spend several nights there and then move on. The vast majority of people I met were determined to return home once the war was over. But they had made it to Poland and many would have liked to stay there while the war was raging. Poland was familiar; it has cultural and historical ties with Ukraine, especially with the western part of Ukraine.

In the post-Soviet times, before this war, thousands of Ukrainians had gone to Poland for work: a member of the European Union, Polish standards of living and salaries were higher than Ukrainian. But Poland was struggling: in the very first months of war it took in about two million fugitives. Posters in the refugee centre read in Ukrainian: "We are happy to welcome you, but our cities are full. Our small rural communities are cozy and peaceful. Consider moving there."

The women who arrived at the refugee centre accepted with resignation the fact that they would have to be on the move again. The way they decided where to go next somewhat surprised me. It wasn't on the basis of a better financial package or living conditions. Rather, the criterion was proximity to Ukraine. The first question that women asked me about various countries also seemed unusual: they wanted to know if they would be able to find work quickly. I would talk about the hardships they had just endured; the necessity to rest, to look around first. But that didn't register. They had worked all their lives, they assured me. They are a hard-working people.

Living at somebody's expenses seemed to them morally reprehensible.

Most of the Ukrainian women I met were mild-mannered and perhaps less assertive, less forceful, compared to North American ones. All were both surprised and grateful for the help and goodwill they'd seen from so many. All were deeply touched by the smallest acts of kindness. And none took the help for granted.

2. My First Bus – Vera and Anna

March 21, 2022 (Korzcowa, Poland) – May 15, 2022
(Vancouver, Canada)

I'M NOT SURE WHY I've singled out Vera, out of so many. Was it the aura of despondency and resignation I felt about her? The way she sat sideways on a chair against the wall, staring fixedly at her clasped hands, alone in a place filled with hundreds of strangers?

I learned that she and her daughter lived in Novo Vodolaga in the Kharkiv region, a predominantly Russian-speaking city, 40 km away from the Russian border. The city and villages around it were heavily shelled, but at the moment of evacuation their houses were still standing.

In her late seventies, Vera was wearing a raincoat and a knitted mohair dome-like cap on her head, the way older people from the provinces used to dress in the Soviet times, seventy years ago or so.

The Soviet textile industry insisted on mousy be-invisible modesty, for all 140 million inhabitants of the USSR. A limited choice of colours, in the unspoken prescriptions of the Soviet dressing code, had to match:

grey to grey, brown to brown, black to black: a grey knitted cap would call for a grey knitted scarf tucked neatly, in a V shape, under the lapels of your coat. Vera had a brown cap on her head but no matching scarf. It was her bare neck that somehow bothered me. I imagined her rushed evacuation, things scattered around, documents, medications randomly pushed into a hand bag refusing to shut ... Now and then she was touching her neck and I thought she was cold.

I asked if I could help her in any way. Did she need clothing, food, or a scarf maybe, to replace the missing, matching one? She shook her head, barely looking at me.

Did she know where she was going, I asked.

"Talk to my daughter. She'll be back soon."

The daughter, Anna, was a tall gaunt woman in her 50s, missing all of her upper teeth.

"Well?" her mother asked.

"Nothing so far."

"Where would you like to go? Any relatives or friends anywhere?"

"No, nobody. My son's back home. Fighting in the army. My mother has left her sister there, my aunt. That's all we have."

"Poland is now full, you see. But there are some other options ..."

"Ah, she doesn't want to go anywhere," Anna said, pointing to her mother with a nod of her head.

"Does she want to stay in Poland, then?"

"No, she wants to go back home. That's all she wants."

"When the war is over, you'll go back. But for now, at least, you are safe here. Both of you."

"I'm a traitor," Vera said. "That's who I am. A traitor."

"A traitor?"

"Yes, I left my sister behind."

The word itself and the way she said it, startled me. It was straight from Stalin's playbook of the 30s and 40s: traitors, saboteurs, murderers. Vera must have absorbed this term with her mother's milk, as they say.

"Our country doesn't need traitors. It will spit them like flies out of its mouth," Putin promised to his nodding audience. This single word brought to my mind the stylistic similarities between the two dictators. And it gave me chills.

"My freezer's full of meats. I need to go home," Vera repeated mechanically.

"Wait till the war is over," I said. "Then you'll return. Ukraine will be rebuilt, you'll see."

Vera gave me a sideways glance.

"Wars do end."

That's the only platitude I could come up with, hardly a consolation at this place and in this time. But what I really thought I couldn't and didn't want to say.

I didn't want to tell her that there was little chance her house would withstand the rocket and bomb attacks aimed at civilians. That pulverized cities and thousands of dead mean nothing to Putin whose goal is to destroy and enslave her country.

I listened to his speech on the eve of his invasion of Ukraine. One authentic sentiment slipped through a wall of well-rehearsed lies: his hatred of Ukrainians. He couldn't hide it, so visceral it was. As far as Putin was concerned, Ukraine had never been a sovereign nation with its own language, history and culture. It's true that for most of the 20th century Ukraine was under Soviet rule. Called *Malorussia* (literally, small Russia), it had been divided between the Russian and Austro-Hungarian Empire in the 19th century.

The fact that in the last 30 years Ukraine had existed as a sovereign state and a burgeoning democracy was a bone in Putin's throat. But his plan of taking over the whole country has failed. A victory parade in Kiev, a symbol of huge significance to him, was not to be. That Putin was preparing for such a parade is now evidenced by full-dress uniforms for the event found in the backpacks of Russian soldiers, killed near Kiev.

"You're safe here; both of you are safe," I said. "But this is just a transit point. Let's look at where you can go from here."

"Safe? But what about my sister? I left her behind."

"She is like this all the time, my Mom! I just can't get her off it," Anna said. "Please help us! Talk to her."

"Let's see ... Did your sister want to come along with you?" I asked.

"That's the whole point! She refused."

"You asked her, right? You really, really tried to persuade her?"

"Oh God, did we ever. I kept pressing – to no avail. And then I left. I'm a traitor."

I was tempted to tell Vera that, as an adult, her sister was a free agent, with a free will and a free choice. But I cut myself short. In the context of the raging war, it would have been as wrong as reminding somebody lost in the desert that there are many beautiful beaches and rain forests in this world.

I asked why the sister had refused to go along with them.

"Oh, her legs are all swollen."

"It's just a pretext, they are not so bad!" Anna exclaimed. "You want to know the real reason she stayed?" She gave a brusque look to her mother. "My aunt thinks she is some kind of a queen. She wants to be served. And who is going to serve her in a refugee camp? So she stayed."

"But now that you're gone who is going to help her?"

"I wouldn't worry about that! There are two neighbours; they'll look after her and our cat."

"Well, then! She is not abandoned. Now let me tell you something: there are countries that really want to welcome you. There are people who will open their homes for you, happily so."

The two women looked at each other.

"But why? We're strangers ..."

"People want to help, that's all ... I guess some want to kill, others to help. Look, you didn't harm anybody, yet are being brutally attacked."

"No, no we didn't do any wrong! Our neighbours, we all lived in peace. Believe us, we're not Nazis. You ask anybody, we are not Nazis!"

"Of course not. The world knows! It feels for you. It stands by you. And it wants to help. There are kind people out there. It's all right, really all right to accept. You'll be all right. You'll see."

Vera turned her face towards me. For the first time her eyes didn't avoid mine.

As the war in Ukraine keeps raging, the counties of European Union have opened their doors and hearts to Ukrainian refugees. On March 4, the Council of the European Union authorized an exceptional measure called Temporary Protection for the displaced people of Ukraine. And now most European counties are offering similar arrangements, temporary protection statutes and residence permits over two to three years; financial assistance; the right to work; free medical care; free education for children; free schools and university; free language courses.

I was lucky to have run into Mark. Slim, clean-shaven, with dark hair and attentive dark eyes, this 25 year-old Danish student of electrical engineering was always there, at the information centre.

As I got to know him better, I asked him why he was working (or rather "serving", as it was called there) in a refugee centre from 9 am until 10 pm, every day for almost a month, sleeping in a cot, with no access to a shower, grabbing a cup of coffee on the go.

When the war began, Mark told me, trouble-shooting electrical system errors stopped making sense to him. Engineering was a respected profession that would earn him money in the future, but history was what he loved most. And history was being made here and now, in Europe, in this refugee centre. He needed to be part of it, he said. Above all, and most importantly, he personally hated Putin and wanted to counteract, in any way he could, the evil the dictator had unleashed.

Working together as an efficient team, Mark and I went on sending several hundreds refugees to Denmark.

The Danish Government promised to welcome 150,00 refugees. At the beginning of April 2022, the country had accepted 30,000: there was space and there were resources for many more. A database was created on Facebook of people who were willing to host the refugee families. People of all walks of life. Young parents with kids who wanted to take in a woman with kids from Ukraine. Older, retired, comfortable couples, whose children were out of the nest, with a basement or an additional room free.

"Where is Denmark?" Vera asked when I brought Mark in to join us.

Mark pulled up a map of Denmark on his phone.

"This is Denmark. Most likely you'll go to Jutland. It's a big peninsula. You may even end up living near the North Sea. Nice climate. Not too hot in summer and not too cold in winter. Though it does snow."

"We are used to snow," Anna said quietly. "Is it ... I mean ... is it a nice country, you think?"

"Very nice!" I rushed to assure her. "Remember Hans Christian Andersen?"

"You mean, the fairy tales? Oh, yeah, my son loved them when he was small."

"He was Danish, Andersen. I went to see the house he was born in. They made a museum around it."

"A big house?" Anna asked.

"No, very small. But all covered with roses."

"We had our little garden too ... grew what we needed," Vera said. "Had a small potato patch. We are kind of used

23

to eat potatoes a lot, you see. Do they grow potatoes in Denmark, you think?"

"My mother needs medication," Anna said. "Will there be a pharmacy where we will live?"

"And how long will be a trip?" asked Vera.

"About seventeen hours."

"That's a long one," Vera said, sighing.

"Yes, but there'll be food on a bus. And the seats are comfortable. You can lean back ..."

"Food," Anna said pensively. "See what happened to me? Don't translate this to the young man." Turning slightly to the side, she pointed to her mouth. "I went to Moscow to have all the nice dentures made. All my savings went to that! I was just about to go back to pick up my dentures when they started the war. What to do? I can't really eat much, only baby food. I don't know how I'll manage."

"Will they let us go back home, that's what I want to know?" Vera said firmly.

That was the question Mark and I heard again and again. Will "they" allow us back? And every time it took Mark by surprise. I knew where these women were coming from. Ukraine became independent from the Soviet Union 30 years ago, recently in historical terms. The older generation grew up under the Soviet rule, which didn't give its citizens any choice as to where they wanted to live, or the liberty to move around at will. Many of the older generation never travelled: you live and die where you were born.

I tried, but I don't think I could really bring it home for Mark. And there was yet another concern he couldn't comprehend.

"Will we be able to stay in the country if we choose to? Or will they evict us?" some younger women with children asked.

"Nobody will evict you! If you have a visa you have the right to stay."

On that day, I made my first list of refugees going to Denmark.

It was a short one: Vera, Anna and three others.

The bus had been in Germany and was on its way to Denmark when Mark called the driver saying he had a few refugees willing to go to Denmark. The driver turned around to pick them up. It was dark by the time the bus reached Poland.

And so I was seeing them off; watching the driver fitting their meagre worldly possessions, their backpacks and bags, into the belly of his bus.

Two more drivers in navy uniforms stepped into the bus. They would be taking turns on the long journey through Europe. A translator on board was there to tell the refugees what it was thought they needed to know.

Mark stepped into the bus to say good-by. I went in to wish my little group easy travel. Happy beginnings. Happy life in a new country.

It was hard for me to speak. Our paths had crossed just for a brief moment in our lives, and during this brief period they became ... family. This family was now leaving.

I saw Vera in the second row, on the left, behind a plate or oranges and apples; in her clumsy coat, and funny cap, her neck still exposed. For the first time her face was relaxed with flashes of anticipation and curiosity.

And so the bus went into the night carrying them through dark fields, forests and towns of Germany, to Hans Christian Andersen's magical land.

To its peace and freedom.

3. Where is America?

March 27, 2022 (Korczowa) – June 1, 2022 (Vancouver)

"WE ARE FROM CHERNIHOV, that hell ... Arrived 3 days ago ..."

Olena could hardly talk.

Chernihov, in the north of Ukraine, was attacked by the Russians on the first day of the invasion. It was an ancient city with beautiful churches, monasteries, and historical buildings. On February 24th, the Russians laid siege to it, just as eighty years earlier the Germans had laid siege to Leningrad. During more than a month, the Russians harassed, tortured and killed its inhabitants. By the time the Russians had retreated, the city lay in ruins. Seven hundred of its inhabitants were dead.

Amidst so many horror stories, that of the bread truck stuck in my memory like a shell shard. With the atrocities committed all over Ukraine, at the time, I didn't pay attention to the location of that one. A truck loaded with bread was allowed by Russians into the city. Russians encouraged women and children to form a line, then opened fire on them.

That, I learned from Olena, had also happened in Chernihov.

The majority of Ukrainians are bilingual: they speak both Ukrainian and Russian with equal ease.

Unlike most wars in history (except civil wars), in this one the invaders could threaten and coerce the invaded in the same language. Were these Russian soldiers joking before opening fire on women and children?

"Take this," I said, handing Olena some cash.

Unlike most, she accepted 100 euros without any argument, quickly hiding the money somewhere on her chest between the folds of her clothing.

As so often, that caused tears:

"Help me, I beg you! Please help me! I'm at my wit's end with him. We're heading to Finland. I have to deliver him safe and sound to his mother, but he keeps running away from me. Hiding. I don't know what he'll do next. Says he hates me. Says it's all my fault!"

"When are you leaving for Finland?"

"In two hours, they say. Waiting for a bus now. You see, my daughter-in-law, she managed to escape with his brothers, my three other grandchildren. We started out all together, six of us. Kolya, don't you dare! Stay close to me! You hear me? Stay close, so that I can see you! So we were finally getting on a bus, with four kids. They've just opened the corridor and it was a real chaos. I'm not that young any more, you see, I had no strength to elbow my way in; we were literally squeezed out; separated from my daughter-in-law and my other grandchildren; I panicked. Our suitcase, I managed to push it in first, and it was gone. I don't know if Olga would recognize it. With three children on a crammed bus ... there is no chance. Well, we have nothing now."

Olena spread her hands in bewilderment.

"I wanted to get back home to wait there for the next bus, but it was too dangerous ... I stayed with a friend ... she gave me a sweater for Kolya. Here I picked up this."

She pointed to an oversized cardigan she was wearing.

"For the next bus, we had to wait for 3 days ... There was still heavy fighting at the outskirts. And this one (she pointed to her grandson standing some distance away from her), he wanted to go with his brothers and his mother. Now he blames me for what happened. Why did they go and I'm stuck with you here, that's what he says. He just doesn't understand. Can you put some sense into his head? Talk to him, please!"

"Speak a little slower, Kolya, will you? Some Ukrainian words I forgot," I said to a small, emaciated 12-year-old. I noticed a strange movement he was making with his tongue: he'd thrust it out, scoop some air and only then form a phrase.

"Don't you know Ukrainian?" he asked.

"Well, it's been a long time since I used it."

"I'm not going to speak Russian to you though," Kolya replied in pure Russian.

"Fair enough. If you don't like my Ukrainian, let's speak some other language then. English, for example."

"I don't know English."

"Not a problem! We can switch over to French."

"You know French?"

"Don't you? How about we try Italian! I'm going to speak Italian to you."

29

Again Kolya thrust his tongue forward, lapping up some air.

"Hmm! I don't know your Italian. Your Ukrainian is really funny though."

"You can correct my mistakes. I'll speak better then."

"You speak Finnish too? That's what they speak in Finland."

"Unfortunately, I don't. It's a difficult language. And you know what's interesting? It has almost no relatives. Finnish is more like an orphan."

"How do you mean?"

"You've got brothers, right? You are a family. Languages too form families. Some are close relatives, some are remote. If you learn one language, it will be easier for you to understand another. If you know Spanish, you'll recognize some words in Italian or French. But with Finnish, it's a different story. Finnish has very few relatives. Estonian maybe ... let's say, its third cousin. Some similarities with Hungarian, but that's about it. And it's a hard one to learn."

"Then I'm not going to learn it."

"Why not? Isn't if fun to learn something that few people know? Especially if you're going to live in Finland?"

"Have you been to Finland?"

"No, but I always wanted to. Will you invite me when you settle there?"

"You're a stranger, why would I invite you?"

"But who has invited you and your whole family? They don't know you, do they?"

"We are *біженці*.[1] We're running away. That's why."

"So you've been running away from rockets and now you're trying to run away from your grandmother. How good is that?"

"She wants me to sit next to her all the time. That's boring. Also, she keeps arguing with me. Herself, she doesn't know anything."

"She must know something, though, don't you think?

"I like geography. But she knows nothing about it. She tells me that America is in Europe. And I'm telling her America is in America. But she won't believe me. "

"You mean the United States? You're right on that one. What are you going to do though? You still have to travel together with your granny. She says you call her names. You not doing that, are you?"

"I don't call her names. I just say she doesn't know anything. That she is *neviglas*."

"*Neviglas*? Ignoramus? Is that what you call her? If somebody kept telling you that you don't know anything, that you are a *neviglas,* how would you feel about it?"

"I'll knock them out, like that." And he threw out a hook in the air with his right hand.

"Look, I've got something for you!" I fumbled in my backpack: books in Ukrainian for small children, crayons, toothbrushes, Tylenols, and at the very bottom, a Rubik's Cube. It belonged to my son years ago, when he

---

1 біженці in Ukrainian translates as "refugees", but literally it means "people on the run".

was Kolya's age. I kept it all these years and now brought it to Poland.

"If you get bored, you can work on this ... on your way to Finland. You're so bright, I'm sure you can figure it out. And then you can write to me from Finland how you did it!"

"I'm not going to write to you because you probably can't even read in Ukrainian!"

He snatched the Rubik's Cube out of my hands, turned around and was gone.

"Kolya, did you say 'thank you'?" his grandma shouted trying to grab him by his arm.

A new flux of refugees poured into the room and soon I lost sight of both of them.

4. The Ghost: Tatyana and Katerina

April 2, 2022 (Korczowa)

THE FOCAL POINT of the Korczowa transit refugee centre was a large area opening to a bus stop with busses evacuating people across Poland and Europe. It had the feel of a train station waiting room marking the end of the escapees' perilous journey through Ukraine to the Polish border, and the beginning of a new, safe one, into the unknown.

People, some sitting, but most standing in groups, their meagre possessions at hand, listened intently to a loudspeaker announcing in Ukrainian: "A bus to Przemysl boarding in half an hour. A bus to Germany. Leaving in an hour."

In the centre of the room, five or six volunteers speaking Ukrainian, Russian, Polish, English, were standing side-by-side behind the desks arranged in a U-shape and swarmed by refugees. With maps of Poland and Europe spread in front of them, volunteers pointed to different cities and explained to the refugees how to get there.

Flags of European countries on the walls announced Europe's readiness to welcome Ukrainians.

But the "railway station" waiting room was never intended to be a communal bedroom.

To enter that hall one morning and to see the ocean of folding cots everywhere I looked, surrounding the information desk island on all sides, was staggering. People fully dressed and wrapped in blankets were just waking up. Some were still sleeping, others sitting in their cots staring in front of them.

Several buses of refugees must have unloaded here during the night. I didn't need to check the news: the proof of the second Russian offensive on the East was in front of my own eyes.

About ten Polish police officers in black uniforms stood shoulder to shoulder behind free desks on the right side, carefully examining the credentials of bus drivers volunteering to take refugees to various destinations. Drivers, mostly men but some women, waited patiently in a long line. They came here from all over the world.

The Korczowa centre was well protected by several layers of security. Police officers and men in fatigues with *stróż* ("guard") written in Polish on the back of their blue jackets patrolled the hallways.

I once tried to take a picture of Americans dancing between the cots and the information desks island. They glided smoothly on the floor wrapping and unwrapping themselves in yellow-blue sheets representing the Ukrainian flag. With faces rumpled by an uneasy sleep, refugees looked on at performers in bewilderment. There was an obvious discrepancy between their present situation and this well intended but rather naive demonstration of solidarity. Still I wanted to film the dancers. A tall man in plain clothing made a decisive step towards me, flicked open his jacket revealing a badge and gestured me to stop. Taking pictures in a refugee centre was not allowed.

A burly driver who must have already had his credentials checked, with a sign "Luxembourg" in hand boomed in Ukrainian:

"Luxembourg! Who is coming with me to Luxembourg? An excellent country, no kidding!"

To everybody who was willing to listen he explained that he was from Ukraine; had been living in Luxembourg for six years and loved it.

Two sisters, with thickly tattooed eyebrows, approached the man. The older – with crude features of her expressive, determined face, and a large, generous body, and the younger, short and thin, with delicate, bird-like features – hardly resembled each other:

"Luxembourg? Never heard of it. We are five of us. She has one kid and those two are mine," the older said with determination. "Are things expensive in your Luxembourg?"

"Sure. The better the life, the higher the prices. But what's your worry? You'll get money from the Government."

"Government? We don't live off anybody's back. I'm a crane operator. She is a painter-plasterer, hard working people. You think there would be work for us in your Luxembourg?"

"That I don't know. All I know, those who want jobs, find jobs."

"What kind of money do they give? Would that be enough for cigarettes, say?" the older sister, who gave her name as Tatyana, asked.

"Cigarettes? You should quit smoking, lady. Cigarettes are expensive."

Tatyana shot a fiery glance at the man: "Advice is cheap!"

"I'm just giving you my opinion."

"Honest to God we've tried!" the youngest, giving her name as Katerina, stepped in. "Tried to quit before the war. But when the war started – oh, God, it made it all worse! Now we smoke like chimneys."

She hid her high-pitched giggle in her elbow.

Tatyana gave a stern look to Katerina.

"If we go, will we be hosted by the same family – all together, with our kids?" Katerina asked.

"Hmm ...what's wrong with living separately, close by? Luxembourg is a small country."

"Oh no!" Katerina said, sly twinkle in her eyes quickly replaced by fear. "I can't make a step without her. She is my brain, my everything!"

"Make up your minds, ladies. I'm leaving soon. Luxembourg. Who wants to go to Luxembourg?"

As far as I could see, his recruiting campaign wasn't successful. Refugees were ready to go to Germany because many had gone there before, and the word spread. As for Luxembourg, that was buying a 'cat in a bag', as the saying goes. An unknown entity.

The two sisters stepped aside to consult.

"We want to stay in Poland," Tatyana said to me firmly. "Nobody wants Ukrainians in Europe, that's for sure. They call us swine there. We're littering the whole of Europe with garbage, that's what they say. They'll take us in, then kick us out next day, just to humiliate."

"Where did you get this information?"

"From the internet."

"Can you show me?"

Tatyana flicked through her phone. And there it was. In Russian.

"You can't really believe it, do you? It must be Russian propaganda! Putin's trolls hard at work." I was visibly upset. The sisters noticed it:

"We don't know what to believe! They write on Internet that Europe let us in, in order to steal our children. Rich landlords in Germany keep children as personal slaves. In their dungeons they keep them. We are alone. We have to fend for ourselves and our kids, understand?"

"Yeah, we do ..." Katerina said. "At least, she's got a husband left at home." Katerina nodded towards her sister. "But I have nobody. A single Mom. Raising my daughter on my own."

"You aren't envious of my coward, are you? Better no husband than the one like mine."

"You're too hard on him, Tanya, honest to God!" Katerina said. The tongues of domestic fire were flaring up in front of my eyes.

"I can only imagine how hard it must have been to leave your loved one behind," I said, repeating the same bromide.

"Hard? This bastard? I should've stayed instead of him. More good would come out of that ... I can fight! I know how to handle a gun! He is 41, my hubby. Has served in the army. Now he is getting call-up papers and what does he do? Hides in the basement, with us, women. For three weeks he's been hiding. When we were leaving, he goes: too bad I didn't make you another baby. With the third one, they let men out. Like hell, I'll have another baby with him! When we come back home, that's the last he'll see of me and the kids. A father like that they don't need!"

"What are you saying, Tanya! I know what it's like for a child without a ..."

"Ah, now she goes again! spinning the same yarn ... You better tell Maria what happened to us on a bus!"

"On a bus?" Katerina shook her head. "I don't even want to think about it. If you want, you tell her."

"Well, we finally managed to get on a bus heading towards Lviv. A volunteer driver was taking us ... About fifteen women with children and one elderly couple. Quite old, those two. The man had a cane and the wife was not much better. We pass many check points. But at Konstantynovka, the Russians order us all out. The old ones are holding on to each other, well, we helped them out."

Tatyana took in another gulp of air.

"When they got out, the Russians order the old man to drop his cane and stand straight. But he can't ... swaying like a blade of grass, trying to hold on to his wife but they shoo her away with a rifle stock ... Russians laugh. Kids are quiet, staring, scared. The old man is swinging like that ...thrashing the air with his arms ..."

"Now you tell the rest," she said to her sister after a pause.

The youngest looked at her sister helplessly but couldn't continue for tears.

"Cut it out. Enough already!" Tatyana silenced her sister sternly.

"You tell her, then ..."

"What's there to tell? They are filth! Fucking assholes! They shoot the old man in the leg, like a duck, for fun. He falls and his wife thinks she too is done for, so she drops next to him. Crawls over to him screaming, checking him out, her hands in blood. Her skirt pulled up, and you can see her flannel underwear. The bus driver dashes to get the wife up on her feet, but the Russians threaten him, you get out of here, before we shoot you all."

"What happened to the man?" I asked.

"What happened? We heard several shots when we were driving off. Now you tell me: what did the old man do to them? What did this poor old woman do to them! What? ... And you say I should get back to my husband, do you?"

Perhaps, the most truthful and terrifying description of Stalin's labour camps are found not in Solzhenitsyn, but in Shalamov's short stories, *Kolyma Tales*.

One phrase in the stories I will never forget.

There are lots of things in the camps, the author says, that it's better not to see or know. But if you did see them, it's better for you to die.

As I was listening to Ukrainian refugees in Poland, the ghost of Soviet labour camps stared into my eyes.

5. Dodo the Clown

March 25, 2022 (Korczowa, Poland)

KORCZOWA, A LARGE WAREHOUSE turned into a transition refugee centre, has a point of entry for new arrivals at one end and the point of departure at the other, with buses taking people to different destinations through Poland and Europe. Between those two points are hours and days of waiting.

Stripped of worldly possessions, schedules and obligations, refugees have the surplus of one thing: TIME.

The calamity of evacuation is now replaced by fatigue and lethargy. Refugees are lying on their cots, dozing or staring at their phones. When the ebb of fugitives is low, families put the vacant cots on their sides, enclosing their space as a kind of a corral for some simulacrum of privacy. The collective experience of terror, varying only in details, precludes talking. It will happen later, generations to come. The films will be made, books written. The world will know. But for now: emotions are dulled and driven deep within.

There are a great number of children here, and they are running amok. Ukrainian women usually start their families earlier than women in North America. You often see mothers in their early twenties, with two or three kids.

Children, taciturn and sullen on arrival, shake off their initial stupor, once they enter a brightly lit and decorated children's room. From 9 am to 6 pm, Israeli and Polish volunteers run a program: games, laughter, competitions – and some quiet moments for movies are on offer. In a separate room, there is a ping-pong table for teenagers.

Mothers leave their phone number with volunteers and can be reached any time.

At 6 pm the Program ends but self-styled fun continues. Wheelchairs and walkers amassed in the corner for older or infirm refugees are turned into scooters.

Riding on top, sideways, three kids per one wheelchair, two on top, one pushing, the fun continues late into the night. The sounds of ping-pong and wheelchairs rolling against the tiled floor will be forever associated for me with a refugee centre, with the early months of this war.

I've always loved clowns, but I haven't seen any real ones since my childhood. In Korczowa, there once appeared a team of three. The contrast between the collective pain and the clowns' frolicking was stark and, in some sense, hard to take. But when I saw the kids' happy faces, I knew the idea of clowns in a refugee camp was an ingenious one. The clowns, one in his late sixties, marked a circle (a stage) on the floor with a yellow tape; kids sat outside the tape on blankets. There were no technical tricks here: the simplicity of the old-fashioned slapstick worked: kids laughed, it made them happy. Later I found out that the "clowns" were lawyers, partners of the same firm.

And then, next day, I saw Dodo. I spotted him pushing a shopper's cart, small yellow umbrella and some batons sticking out of it. His white tuxedo with long tails contrasted sharply with a mass of wiry salt-and-pepper hair. Dodo seemed to be in the midst of a ferocious argument with his own umbrella. Wagging his yellow-gloved finger at it, he stopped in front of a cot with a woman with a blank face expressing the greatest degree of gloom. As if puzzled by something, Dodo gesticulated wildly, firing questions at her and anybody around who would agree to listen. It took me a while to realize that Dodo's fiery monologues were nothing but a string of meaningless sounds, so precisely his "speech" imitated the whole range of human emotions – from surprise to disagreement, to nod-nod approval. For some reason, this gobbledygook was hilariously funny.

Fascinated, I kept watching Dodo. Moving his red potato-shaped nose in a funny way, he walked straight up to the woman with a sour face and picked up something from her blanket. It turned out to be a brown puppy, a French bull-dog, that I hadn't noticed before. Its funny bat ears stuck out and deep wrinkles made it look like an old baby.

Holding the puppy in his hands, Dodo addressed the woman in his gibberish. To my surprise, she answered in full honesty, in Ukrainian. With my help they now struck up a conversation!

It turned out that Nina was bed-ridden as a result of a serious car accident three years earlier. How did she, in her condition, together with her teenage son and her husband, manage to escape from Mykolayiv, a port city in the south, attacked by Russians, is a mystery to me. And that was not all.

An in unison and persistent moan came out of four or five cat carriers forming a row along the wall.

"What is it?" I asked Nina.

"My babies. They all came with us. They hear we're having fun and complain that they are excluded."

The 'babies' happened to be five puppies.

It turned out, Nina and her husband were purebred dog breeders. Before the war, they were well-known in their city and beyond.

"I was an accountant before the accident. But I couldn't work any more, so I switched over to dog breeding. We couldn't have left any of them behind, could we? This little one (she pointed to the puppy Dodo was still holding in his hands) is like my baby. Doesn't want to be without me for a minute. Sleeps with me, eats with me. And the other ones are jealous! They complain."

When Dodo moved on to the next batch of refugees, I asked him what his real profession was, in a normal life. I now expected all "clowns" to be retired or semi-retired lawyers.

It was strange, almost disappointing, to see his mouth produce real sounds, of a real language. He spoke English, with an accent that I couldn't place.

"What do you mean 'real profession'? This is my real profession. I'm a clown. I work in Israeli hospitals."

"They don't allow pictures here," I said. "But may I?"

"Sure! As many as you want," Dodo said, putting his arm around my shoulders and striking the prankiest of postures.

And then Dodo the clown moved on, pushing his cart and picking up a new squabble with his umbrella.

6. Tikun Olam

March 30, 2022 (Korczowa) – July 10, 2022 (Vancouver)

If I am only for Myself, What am I?
If not Now, When?
—Hillel

MY MEMORY HASN'T RETAINED the name of that woman: our encounter – at a bus stop – was fleeting. What I do remember is her face.

Refugees I came across didn't usually carry emotions on their sleeves. Most had closed, blank expressions stamped with exhaustion or silent resignation. What I did not expect to see at a refugee centre was a happy, smiling face.

I will call her Natasha, a common name among the women I met. Natasha was beaming with happiness.

Her escape from Kiev looked more like the beginning of a tourist trip rather than an evacuation under dire circumstances. She was an artist heading towards Italy where her Italian friends were supposed to pick her up. Travelling by car with her friend, she planned to stay in Italy for two weeks, visiting some museums and then coming back home.

It was only a day before, that I had noticed somebody else's car parked at the border crossing with the traces of bullets on its side. "Children!" was scrawled in capitals on a piece of paper placed on the windshield.

But Natasha travelled in comfort … till at the very border their car broke down and, instead of driving to the Warsaw airport, Natasha had to cross the border by foot, finding herself in a place she did not expect to be: in a refugee centre.

"I'm so happy I ended up here!" she told me excitedly. "If it were not for that accident, I would not have seen all these amazing things!"

What she meant by "amazing things" was the massive outpouring of goodwill and empathy she witnessed. Natasha's reaction was not unique. The refugees I met were equally surprised that so many people from all over the world had put their regular lives and commitments on hold to be committed to helping them, strangers.

Putin's war unleashed death and destruction, but inadvertently, it has also set free the generosity and kindness that easily stay dormant locked inside the shell of our routine lives. And there it was: thousands of people donating money to the huge humanitarian effort. Thousands of ordinary families in big cities, small towns and villages across the world, rearranging their homes to welcome destitute strangers; readjusting their schedules and budgets; cooking additional meals; setting an extra place at their tables; putting a translator app into their smart phones to communicate with their guests; donating hours of their time by filling out the necessary papers; getting Ukrainian kids to school; helping refugees to find work and adjust to a new life.

What does it take, I wondered, to show such altruism on a short notice, in the times of need? Good heart, empathy, for sure. But also, imagination: the ability to put oneself in the shoes of another. That is exactly what those who order the war and kill are incapable of doing. "Fascists, bad people, not me," these labels wipe out humanity of the other.

The Polish people, at the front line of humanitarian efforts, have welcomed millions of Ukrainians in their homes without any compensation from the state.

The refugee evacuation centre was organized in such a way as to satisfy the major needs (with the exception of a shower) of the thousands who were sheltered there. Volunteers behind the information desks, the heart of the centre, at a drop of a hat became travel agents. They worked tirelessly directing refugees to various destinations and patiently answering hundreds of their questions.

Volunteers representing countries of the European Union coordinated the schedules of buses and helped to match host families with the evacuees. Many bus drivers were also volunteers. I met a volunteer who had come all the way from Australia to drive Ukrainians across Poland in a bus he rented, all at his own expense.

Children ripped out of school by war were at loose ends for weeks. At the centre, the Program for children, essential for their well-being, was also run by volunteers.

On arrival, the evacuees lined up in front of a kiosk where free SIM cards were inserted in their phones by volunteer tech whizzes. It was understood that the first thing people needed would be to notify their families that they had made it to Poland safely.

The World Central Kitchen, an NGO providing meals in humanitarian crises and natural disasters, was feeding evacuees around the clock. On the days of mass exodus, the Kitchen would prepare 60,000 meals a day. To organize food delivery (most coming from Poland, with oranges from Spain), to make thousands of sandwiches, soup and salad portions took an enormous effort. Polish and American volunteers stood long hours behind the counter, enthusiastically filling up wide plastic bowls with vegetable stew and goulash; pouring out tea, coffee, hot chocolate and hot porridge; handing out fruit and sweets to the kids. I saw no signs of fatigue on their faces and was surprised at the easy banter they exchanged after many hours behind the counter. I asked one Pole serving food what made him look so happy under such difficult circumstances. "When hungry people eat, they feel better. That makes me feel better too!" was his answer. And a French chef, at the food stall, outside the centre, bending over an unsmiling child, urging him to take lollipop from his hands. The child stood bewildered in front of a stranger, a foreigner, frowning, hands down. After some cajoling, he finally plucked up his courage, sighed as only the adults would, took the lollipop and smiled.

"C'est ça!" the Frenchman exclaimed. "C'est pour ça que je suis venu ici. Pour voir un enfant sourire!"

"D'où venez-vous?" I asked.

"Marseille."

He came here from Marseille just for that: to see a child smiling.

The evacuee centre in Korczowa was a microcosm reflecting a larger, world-wide effort. At the border crossing in Medyka, I saw representatives of *Fundacja Ocalenie* (the Polish Salvation Foundation); Red Cross; International Sikhs; Jehovah Witnesses; Doctors Without Borders; ION, the International Organization for Migration (part of the United Nations system), supporting migrants all over the world; Japanese Christian charity "No to Hunger"; as well as several Israeli agencies. There, at the border, I talked to a member of a volunteer group whose aim was to deliver to the front-line hygiene supplies for female soldiers of the Ukrainian army.

Inside Ukraine, many Ukrainian volunteer bus drivers drove the escapees to safety, often risking their own lives under falling bombs and rockets. Volunteer Ukrainians sheltered and fed women and children all along the dangerous journey from the east of Ukraine to the west.

After the war, some of the Ukrainians will choose to stay in their host countries. But unlike refugees from Africa or Middle East, most Ukrainians would want to return home. Those who return will bring back first-hand experience of life in established Western democracies. That experience will enrich their lives and contribute to the flourishing of their heroic country, thus achieving the opposite effect intended by the aggressor.

My boss Robert, a former Polish soldier, working for a Jewish organization JDC, that I volunteered for, was not a man of many words.

"I'm looking for a mother and her son."

That's all he said when we drove to Medyka, a border crossing that refugees would cross by foot.

Had I not known what it was, I could have taken Medyka for a Sunday fair, with its gaudy tents on both sides of a passage and various stalls offering free food: "Recognize the Human Race as One" read the sign above the stall with Indian food.

Ukrainian style dumplings and hot dogs were on offer at the stall next to it. Steps away, a volunteer, armed with scissors, was giving a hair cut to a refugee woman sitting on a chair in front of him. "Humanitarian Rescuer," read a sign over his head, both in English and Korean. This man with the scissors was the only one I ever saw with a COVID face mask.

In this unquiet war-time April, the temperatures at the Polish-Ukrainian border were close to zero. Certainly nobody could stay in the tents overnight. Any shelter here would be temporary.

We peeped into several tents before we found the pair we were looking for.

Refugees were sitting silently in a circle on wooden crates. Robert called out the name. A middle-aged woman got to her feet. Robert quickly brought up a photograph on his iPhone. The real face matched the photo. Without any extra words, the mother and her teenaged son followed us to the car. The same day they would be taken to the hotel in Warsaw and, several days later, flown to Israel.

In the car Tatyana, a large, heavy-set woman in her fifties, spilled her greatest fear: she wasn't sure she was Jewish; the whole plan with Israel might collapse, she feared. Her only claim to Jewish identity, she told me, would be her grandmother whose documents had been lost during the Second World War. She remembered that her grandmother was making *latkes*, so she must have been Jewish after all. I shared Tatyana's concerns with Robert: "Tell her not to worry. If JDC said they'd get her to Israel, they will."

JDC (known as Joint) founded more than a hundred years ago, is a global Jewish humanitarian organization with a presence in 70 countries. Their mission is described on their site as follows: "We rescue Jews in danger, provide aid to vulnerable Jews, develop innovative solutions to Israel's most complex social challenges, cultivate a Jewish future, and lead the Jewish community's response to global crises like natural disasters, public health emergencies, and more. In times of crisis, natural disasters, war, famine, JDC offers aid to non-Jews to fulfill the Jewish tenet of *tikkun olam*, the moral responsibility to repair the world and alleviate suffering wherever it exists."

In Poland, JDC had shelters, community centres for refugees, and a whole network of people – Jews and non-Jews – working around the clock on complicated logistics of finding Ukrainians, extracting them from the war-zone, providing for their needs and sending them onto safety, as well as coordinating the efforts of the international team of volunteers. Amidst this huge refugee crisis, the efficiency, the speed and the precision of their work were truly amazing.

While people in the West gave abundantly and willingly, for the Russians – inside and outside Russia – helping the Ukrainians proved illegal and dangerous.

In Moscow and St. Petersburg, a clandestine network was assisting Ukrainians deported to Russia in reaching Western Europe. Russians living outside of Russia would help with the logistics, connect people who could temporarily accommodate the fugitives and often provide money for the tickets on their way to freedom. We know now that the Russians in the occupied territories often force starving Ukrainians to obtain a Russian passport in exchange for food.

Those who were lucky to escape Mariupol before it was bombed and taken over, often did not have any documents on them. Many ended up in Crimea, annexed by Russia in 2014. Now they were trying to get to Western Europe. The only country accepting refugees without any documents was Estonia.

When Putin unleashed the war, thousands of Russian intellectuals, writers, educators, journalists, artists, doctors and engineers left Russia in protest, albeit, by necessity, silent.

Not only did they find themselves without access to their money, work and means of survival, but their Russian passport became an anathema.

The Russian émigrés who had been living in Slovakia before the war and were now organizing a humanitarian effort for Ukrainian refugees, found themselves in cross hairs. The sight of their red passport with a crowned eagle caused suspicion in the eyes of the Slovaks while delegitimizing their activity in the eyes of the Russian government.

As a result, the activists among them were ready to cut links with the country, their homeland, that had unleashed the brutal war.

Since obtaining Slovakian citizenship takes many years (one has to have a continuous permanent residence in the country for at least eight years, immediately preceding the submission), one Russian activist and business woman launched an initiative to replace Russian passports with Nansen ones. Few remember now what a Nansen passport is. And yet, at the pivotal and tragic point of European history, in the aftermath of WWI and the Russian revolution, Nansen passports saved the lives of thousands.

Fridtjof Nansen, the famous arctic explorer, oceanographer and zoologist, turned diplomat, statesman and major humanitarian, winning a Nobel Peace Prize, deserves a separate narrative. What concerns us here is the time in his career when he turned his prodigious energies from Arctic explorations to helping homeless refugees: first to the Russian victims of revolution, civil war and hunger, then to Armenian victims of a genocide.

In 1917, more than 200,000 Russian intellectuals, aristocrats, professionals, and middle-class people fled Communist Russia. Devastated after the war, Europe had neither means nor resources to accommodate them. Without a passport, the escapees had no legal rights anywhere in the world: applying for a job, studying, opening a back account or travelling, proved impossible. Nansen passports didn't return them the country they loved and lost, but it legitimized their existence in 50 countries, members of the Geneva convention. Ultimately 450,000 refugees got the passport.

Among the recipients were Sergey Rakhmaninov, Igor Stravinsky, Vladimir Nabokov and Ivan Bunin, the first Russian Nobel Prize Laureate for literature.

Is history repeating itself now? Tikun Olam.

To Repair the World.

P.S. *October 2, 2022 – Vancouver*

Putin's so-called "partial" mobilization is causing another humanitarian crisis, as hundreds of thousands of men (many with young families) are fleeing Russia to Georgia and Kazakhstan. At the time of this writing, 700,000 had already escaped. Waiting in miles-long lines for days at border crossings, with no food or water, they freeze in the windy steps of eastern Russia and in high altitudes of the mountain passage to Georgia. According to the BBC's Russian service, both in Russia and Kazakhstan, women took the initiative of helping people in crisis. In Russia, Alexandra started a chat on Instagram, called "Women Will Drive You Out." There are more than 700 people registered. She and other women drive men all the way to Kazakhstan and then return to pick up more. Those who managed to cross the border into Kazakhstan are homeless: they are reported to be wandering around not daring to ask locals for help. Yet, they are treated like brothers; many families welcome total strangers in their homes; provide them with food and money donated by the neighbours. Nino, who takes Russians to Stepantsminda, a townlet in the mountains of north-eastern Georgia, has been participating since spring in the project *Emigration for Action,* initially created for Ukrainian refugees. Now they are opening a shelter for fleeing Russians. In Nino's words: "First we thought: Whom shall we admit? I thought there should be some selection criteria. But we couldn't decide which one: Shall we ask them 'Whose is Crimea'? Yet at the border, I saw ordinary people who were simply lost ... I realized it would have been inhumane: everybody had to be admitted."

7. Some Kind of Fish?

April 7, 2022 (Korczowa)

TODAY I MET A POLISH VOLUNTEER looking for two people to help him deliver sanitary items to women soldiers fighting in this war alongside the men. Somehow I thought of men, not women fighting in this bloody war. I was wrong: thousands of women, some on the front line, were battling for the survival of their country. I was tempted to go, but crossing to the war zone with a Canadian passport proved to be next to impossible.

While I was thinking about it, I noticed a middle-aged man was standing outside, next to the departing buses. In a worn-out canvas blazer, extremely emaciated, he was visibly shaking in the gusts of cold wind. The man was holding a half-empty plastic bag, his hands twitching. I asked him if he had any other luggage. He shook his head.

What bus was he waiting for, to what destination? He shrugged his shoulders.

I had observed the expression of silent resignation or fatigue on many faces. I'd seen tears. His face was a face of silent agony, Munch's "The Scream", with a mouth shut. Was he in physical pain?

I offered him Tylenol. No, he said, that won't help. He was using a special medication for tuberculosis. But he had run out of it, he said. He hoped to get more in Sweden.

Sweden?

Yes, that's where his wife and daughter had fled to. All he wanted was to see them before his death, which was imminent, he believed. Not every country would let in refugees with contagious deseases, but Sweden did.

What was the name of the city his family went to?

He couldn't remember. He had managed to talk to his wife once using somebody's phone. Who it was, he didn't remember. His wife gave him her number, he wrote it down on a piece of paper but couldn't find it anywhere: he'd searched in every pocket.

The name of the city sounded like some kind of a fish or *восьминіг*—octopus, he said.

Did he try to talk to some authorities about it, somebody who might help?

Again the man shook his head.

We approached a Polish police officer together. It took about 40 minutes of detective work to determine the city and some more time to find the man's family in it. The city on the Baltic Sea was called Kalmar. By lucky coincidence, its name resembled the Russian word *кальмар,* "squid." But it certainly wasn't Octopus.

The bus to Wroclaw was departing later that day. Then six hours on a ferry across the Baltic Sea, and then – Sweden.

I'm sure Sweden would provide him with needed medication. In combination with the love of the finally-found family, could it give him new licence on life?

I do want to believe it!

8. Semper Augustus: Kristina and Lydia

April 8, 2022 (Korczowa) – June 2, 2022 (Vancouver)

Petite, of a delicate build, Kristina stood alone at the bus waiting area, next to the wall, away from the crowd. She held with both hands in front of her a medium size duffer bag, all she had.

Most refugees were dressed for the hazards of the escape; in pieces picked out of *humanitarka* heaps dotting different stops on their route to safety. But Kristina's clothing was well-cut and neat: a beige jacket with a matching turtle neck, a little scarf; and dress trousers of a darker tone.

When I began to talk to her, she answered sparingly, in monotone. Her world seemed to be closed on itself: nor did she look at me, but above my face, with a concentrated, dry eye, as if she saw something I couldn't access. From time to time, as if returning from her world, she'd move her eyes to meet mine but only for a brief moment. I didn't register much in her world, that much was clear.

I wanted to give her some money, but didn't dare, afraid it might somehow humiliate her.

Our conversation didn't play out well. Yet, I wasn't getting signals from her that I should leave either, so I dallied, undecided.

Finally, out of the sparse bits she divulged, I managed to assemble the picture of what had happened: Kristina, it turned out, was alone in the world with no home left: the rocket had hit her house when she stepped out for several hours. Children? No.

Actually, yes, thirty of them. Yes, all mine.

Turned out Kristina had been a Director of an orphanage for a quarter of a century. Several months before the war she had retired. Yet, on that fateful day, she went over to lend a hand packing the kids: the arrangements had been made to evacuate the orphanage to Austria. It was at this time that a rocket hit her house. It must have been an errant one, Kristina said, pausing. Their town was in the middle of Ukraine, considered safe; they believed they were evacuating children much in advance.

"How lucky that you survived!" I said dismayed at what I had just heard. Colour rose to her cheeks.

"Lucky? Me, lucky?"

It looked like I had made a serious blunder.

After Kristina had retired she would often bring kids to her place – one at a time, for two or three days, especially those who had health problems.

"They needed a little break, the orphans, different food, and a sense of home," she said.

Lydia was a fifteen-year-old whose ulcer had been exacerbated by war. She didn't feel well and asked to stay at Kristina's place for one last night before the evacuation to Austria. Kristina needed to pick up something at the orphanage. Lydia stayed back waiting for her to return.

We both fell silent. I watched the chaotic movement of people; going in and out, in and out.

I wondered why Kristina hadn't left for Austria together with her former charges after her house had been bombed.

"They aren't my charges any more," she replied. "I'm retired. They have a new director: I don't want to be the fifth wheel in a carriage ... And besides ... how can I face these kids after what had happened? I buried Lydia. She didn't have anybody except me."

Kristina stayed alone in the empty orphanage building for three weeks. Till more rockets rained on her town.

"Now I'm here," she said, avoiding looking at me. "Don't know what for. She is alive and I'm dead."

Has she misspoken, I wondered. If that was a 'Freudian slip,' it so nakedly exposed the way Kristina felt.

"What country are you going to?"

"Holland."

"Anybody there?"

"No. They put people in evacuation centres there, I've heard. If I'm lucky, in some hotels. But it doesn't make any difference to me now. None whatsoever. I'm going for her ... Lydia always wanted to go to Holland, you see. I had a little garden, and we were growing all kinds of things, but especially tulips. That was her passion, tulips. She hoped to become a horticulturalist when she ... when she grows up ..."

Kristina paused, then, with an effort, said: "Her favourites were those black ones, called Queen of Night. Wait, I'll show you."

She pulled an iPhone out of her pouch, and pointed to a little patch of richly purple, almost black, tulips.

"For me, they were too funereal. But she thought they were exceptional. Said real black didn't exist in nature, maybe that's what intrigued her. But let me show you something else."

Lydia flicked to the next picture: crimson flowers with variegated petals seemed to have absorbed all the sunlight in the world, so festive and bright they looked.

"These look like Semper Augustus, but they are not. Do you know anything about Semper Augustus?"

For the first time I saw lively sparks in Kristina's eyes.

"The real Semper Augustus doesn't exist any more. See these veins, like tongues of white flame? It was a virus that made Semper Augustus so beautiful. And the Dutch went crazy. One bulb had cost the price of a house in the 17th century. I didn't know any of that either: my girl told me. She read all the books, knew everything there was to know about tulips. There is a tulip museum in Amsterdam she wanted to visit."

"Hopefully it will work for you in Holland. But in case it doesn't, for some reason, you can move to another European country, you know that?"

"I think one move will be too many. But thank you anyway for talking to me."

And without looking at me, Kristina turned around and walked away.

I walked my way too, shaken by her story. Then I stopped abruptly, thinking I should return and offer her some cash.

To this day I regret I didn't have the courage.

9. I Saw Their Faces:
Oleg, Oksana, Jaroslav

April 9, 2022 (Korczowa) – August 11, 2022
(Vancouver, Canada)

ONE THING PUZZLED ME: while a huge flow of refugees was pouring into Europe, a smaller but substantial
counter current was going in the opposite direction, back
home, to Ukraine. That was happening in spite of the
escalating war; in spite of continuing bombing of every
major city; in spite of the sadistic butchery unleashed by
Putin's soldiers of which the refugees were aware.

And when it came to evacuation, out of 12 million
displaced (at the time of this writing), only 5 per cent
did so when the government urged them to. The other 95
percent fled when the danger was imminent.

Ukrainians are known for their strong attachment
to their land, their homes, their way of life. The fierce
bravery of Ukrainian warriors withstanding the Russian
Moloch has been proving that every day.

But the less abstract and more immediate reason for wanting to go back, no matter the danger, was that every family was torn apart. Males between 18 to 60 had to stay back to defend their country. The desire to reunite with the loved ones for many was stronger than the fear of rockets.

Before discussing any relocation to a host country I had to reassure the destitute that they would be able to return home any time they wished: after the war, even during the war, if they so chose.

Adjusting to new cultures and languages proved to be an insurmountable difficulty especially for older people; for people from rural areas who had never left their villages before.

Of all the refugees I came across, only one didn't want to return home.

I met Oleg as he walked past massive wooden crates that formed a makeshift corridor through which refugees filed into Korczowa refugee centre, having crossed the border by bus. Like many others, Oleg ignored the leaflets scattered on top of the crates. At the end of a long journey through a war-torn country, many preferred to receive information about the available services from a volunteer, face-to-face.

As I approached Oleg, his wife, with a three-month-old baby in her arms and the older girl at her side, quickly looked me over and moved forward, not participating in a conversation.

Oleg, with his well-groomed, handsome, clean-shaven face, was an unusual sight among the crowds of exhausted women with children. His whole figure exuded confidence. But his shrewd, dark eyes scrutinized me with an undisguised mistrust. The more I talked, the more suspiciously he looked at me. Are you trying to sell me something? What is there for you in all of this? Those were his unuttered but easily discernible questions.

Was it the nature of this man, I wondered, or the wartime hardships he had endured that urged him to build the wall between himself and another human being?

I told him where he could find me if needed, and started to walk away. My strategy worked. He nodded to his wife to wait, and quickly caught up with me.

As with so many, he needed to figure out what to do next, where to go.

But I was cautious: "Depends on your goals. If you want to return as soon as the war ends, perhaps staying close to Ukrainian borders is a good idea. Slovakia? Lithuania? Other Baltic states? They all accept Ukrainians." (I avoided the word refugees).

"No," Oleg said firmly. "I'm not planning to return. Ukraine is corrupt. Oligarchs got all the power, but the middle class has no chance. Zelensky promised to get rid of oligarchs but did nothing."

That was unexpected. Usually refugees didn't discuss politics.

"He tried hard to fight corruption before the war, that's what I heard. Maybe he hasn't fully succeeded ... He is a true leader of the nation now, a man of great courage, don't you think?"

"Oh yeah, the war has saved his face. But I didn't vote for him. I voted for Poroshenko[2]. Whom Zelensky put on trial because he was his rival."

"Didn't Zelensky drop all charges against Poroshenko in the time of war? And didn't they shake hands and Poroshenko promised to do all he could with the war efforts?"

For the first time Oleg looked at me with some interest.

"Zelensky surrounded himself with his kin. His own people. Actors, television people. You think it's right? In a country that is supposed to be a democracy?"

"I think in the time of war you need people you can trust. People who are tested."

"Politics stinks. I'm glad I've left. Right now I'd like to find a country that would need my skills. I'm very good at what I'm doing."

It turned out he designed dress shoes for women. He loved his profession and hoped to continue working in his field in some "good European county," as he put it.

When I brought up the possibility of Denmark, his eyes again pricked me with suspicion.

I'm just sharing information, I heard myself saying. The choice is entirely yours. Oleg's questions about Denmark differed from that of others. Women would first inquire about schools and kindergartens for their children; then about the possibility of work for themselves. The idea that they should give themselves some time to recuperate from trauma or simply rest didn't seem to enter

---

2   Poroshenko is a Ukrainian businessman and politician who served as the fifth president of Ukraine from 2014 to 2019.

their minds. But once you assured them that the financial support would be enough to provide for their needs, women rarely asked specific questions about the size of that support.

Not so with Oleg. Some of his pointed questions neither Mark, an electrical engineer, turned volunteer, and less so I, could answer.

How much per day will I get?

Hard to say. Every municipality pays differently, depending on the cost of living, Mark explained.

What is the purchasing value of Danish crone compared to Ukrainian grivna? Mark pulled out his calculator. Then made several calls to Denmark.

What if we dislike the host family or they dislike us?

The community will try to find you some other family.

And if that doesn't work out either?

Another attempt will be made.

And if that fails as well?

They'll try to find you a separate apartment, then.

In hindsight Oleg's nit-picking is understandable. He had a wife, a baby and an older daughter to take care of. Later when he relaxed, changed into a jump suit, and some friendly notes appeared in his voice, he told me that he had another child in Ukraine, being raised by his first wife. That explained why he could leave Ukraine, he said. Fathers of three children were exempt.

Only when his family was put on a list of people going to Denmark did Oleg tell me about his next concern: his car. They managed to leave Ukraine in their own car and he wanted to continue driving though Europe – he'd find some hotel to stay overnight.

Money?

Not a problem, he had enough, he said.

Leaving the car at the centre was possible, but he was reluctant to do that.

"You can go by car," Mark said. "But then you'll be on your own; we won't be able to help you."

Several weeks after arrival, Oleg texted me: "The journey on a bus was difficult. Holding the baby in our arms all the way was inconvenient. Both girls got running noses. The hosts are nice people but four of us are sleeping in the same large room. The town is small with nothing interesting in it. The future is unclear."

* * *

"My mother was afraid they won't let me cross the border. They thought I was eighteen."

Tall and well-build, at fifteen, Yaroslav resembled a proverbial knight from Slavic folklore: it was easy to imagine him freeing princesses from captivity while fighting the dragon. Yet there was an air of serenity and gentleness about this young boy. For a fifteen-year-old he was surprisingly well-mannered and polite.

His mother eyed Yaroslav gravely without saying a word.

Everything about Oksana was ash-pale: her skin, her hair, her eyes.

"Mom wants to go back home," Yaroslav said. "Talking about it all the time."

There was no irritation in his soft voice, just an echo of regret.

They'd just arrived and I showed them the cafeteria.

"She won't eat anything, my mother," Yaroslav said.

"How about some tea or coffee? You'll feel better then," I said, turning to Oksana. She nodded, her eyes downcast.

"What to do with our suitcase?" Yaroslav asked. "Can we leave it somewhere?"

"I never heard of people stealing here. But to be on the safe side, better not to leave things unattended. I'll keep an eye on your stuff while you're getting food."

I moved closer to our table a small suitcase and Yaroslav's backpack: the only possessions my charges had.

Yaroslav went over to the counter – his mother didn't seem to have any strength or motivation to move.

When I tried to talk to her, she spoke reluctantly, in monotone. They were from Kharkiv. Their flat had been intact when they left. But there was nobody to look after it.

Perhaps they could have stayed. She pulled a handkerchief somewhere from the sleeve of her coat and wiped her eyes.

"If you need any clothes, I can show you later where donated coats, sweaters, scarves, and warm hats are," I said.

Oksana shook her head. No, they didn't need anything.

She hoped their apartment in Kharkiv would not be bombed.

Kharkiv. So deadly the Russian attack on that city was that President Zelensky compared the battle of Kharkiv with the battle of Stalingrad in WWII. By the beginning of March, 600,000 of Kharkiv's inhabitants had been evacuated. Oksana and her son had not been among them. They stayed another three weeks.

Second-largest, mostly Russian-speaking city in Ukraine and briefly its capital, Kharkiv is a city of baroque architecture, theatres, world class museums, libraries and educational and research institutions. It's also a powerful industrial hub with factories and plants numbering in the hundreds. It's as strategically important for Putin as it was for Nazi Germany 80 years ago when the Wehrmacht took over the city and kept it under brutal occupation for two years. Three battles and half a million soldiers' lives later, the Russian army was able to liberate Kharkiv. Now the Russians were bombing and shelling that very city, killing the civilians that their great-grandfathers had liberated.

During the occupation, the Nazis deported thousands of Kharkiv civilians for slave labour in Germany. Right now, the Russians are deporting Ukrainians to filtration camps in Donetzk and in prisons and labour camps in Siberia and Far East.

"What did you do before the war?" I asked Oksana.

"Worked as a care aid in the nursery. With toddlers. A single mom. Raised Yaroslav alone."

"You sure did a good job. Look what a wonderful young man he is. He really cares about you, I can tell. Must be hard for him to see his mother upset all the time. He is young, he wants to travel. In a way, it's an opportunity for him to see Europe. Perhaps for his sake you could ..."

I didn't finish: Oksana gave me a sidelong glance, my speech obviously at odds with her quiet despair.

"Ukraine will win the war. The world will help Ukraine to rebuild. You'll be able to go back, you'll see!" I was repeating my mantra.

Did I believe what I was saying? With the brutal war expanding, nothing at that point could give me that certainty. But later, unable to fall asleep, I repeated to myself that Ukraine will win and felt comforted by my own conjectures.

I worried about Oksana though and wanted to see her next day first thing in the morning, before anybody else.

Oksana looked as pale and as resigned as the day before. She sat on the edge of the cot, her hands folded in her lap.

On the cot next to hers, Yaroslav was googling information on his phone about different countries I had mentioned the previous day. Every second he was blowing his straight corn-pale bangs off his forehead.

"Your hair must be in your way," I said.

"I haven't washed it for two weeks, that's why. Is there any place to wash?"

"No showers here, unfortunately. Was it quiet here at night? Did your mother sleep OK?"

"Not sure. But I think she did. She is scared all the time. That's the problem."

"May I sit next to you?" I asked Oksana. "Trust me: the worst is behind you. It will only be better from now on."

She shook her head, then raised her pale sorrowful eyes at me. I saw that nothing had registered in them. But I continued to press my point.

"Look, I'm not saying it's going to be easy: some strange country, some strange language; people doing things differently. What I am saying is that you'll meet very kind people, and that, I think, what counts most ... it would for me ..."

"Are you sure?"

"Absolutely! There are huge lists of those who want to take Ukrainians in. Nobody forces them to do it. All over Europe and North America people say: we want to help."

A little later, I was able to take Yaroslav aside.

I told him about my grandfather who had been shell-shocked during WWII. Fatigue, nightmares, headaches, confusion, apathy stayed with him for a long time.

"Your mother is not physically wounded. But she is psychologically shell-shocked. Takes a long time to heal. Somebody has to look after her in the meantime. Looks like she has nobody except you."

"I'm trying," Yaroslav said, sighing. "But I don't know what to say to her ... She is like that all the time ... For me ... I don't mind going somewhere. It would be fun to see some other country, Germany or Denmark or Greenland. I always wanted to see Greenland." He puffed his bangs off his forehead.

"I haven't seen any Greenland representatives here."

"Is Danish a difficult language? I don't particularly like math. But I like languages."

"I think any language is not difficult to pick up just to get by. Shopping, asking directions, that kind of thing. But to know a language in depth, to really master it ... hmm ... that takes a lot of time and effort. Eighty five per cent of Danes speak English though."

"Shall I learn English then?"

I hesitated before speaking:

"I'm sure Ukraine will win the war, and the West will help rebuild your country. There'll be a great demand for specialists in all kinds of fields. In addition to your Ukrainian and Russian, the knowledge of English will open many doors for you. On the other hand ... if you're going to live in Denmark, you should know the language of the country welcoming you, don't you think? Perhaps ... and why not? You are young. You can learn both, Danish and English?"

"I have a translator app. I'll use it in Denmark. You think our hosts will have this app too?"

"Pretty sure."

The bus was departing for Denmark in the late afternoon.

Once again I picked up a hand-written list, found a rare chair to sit on and asked each potential passenger to come over with their Ukrainian passports, that attractive looking piece with a yellow trident on a dark-blue cover granting its owner a special protection all over Europe.

When the bus with Oleg and his wife and daughters, with Yaroslav and Oksana and others had left, Mark came up to me.

He had dark circles under his eyes and didn't look good.

"What am I doing? I'm only 25 years old. What right do I have to change people's lives at he drop of a hat? To choose their destiny for them? Their children may stay in Denmark, marry, have their own children ...they won't be Ukrainians any more."

Unlike Mark, I had no such qualms.

There are rare moments in history when one has to trust one's intuition, one's moral sense and act quickly. Even if all the consequences of the action can't be predicted.

But my high-flying rhetoric didn't quell Mark's doubts. Here on the ground were hundreds of traumatized and destitute women with children talked into taking chances and making a choice between one unknown and the other unknown. Not in a month, in a week. Now.

* * *

I recalled the time I went to Israel to make a documentary about Sugihara, a Japanese consul in Lithuania who issued thousands of visas to Jewish refugees during the Second World War.

I know this comparison is not fair. The Ukrainian refugees are out of danger in Poland. They can choose where to go next. The world has changed since the Second World War. It is welcoming the Ukrainians with the open arms. And neither Mark nor I risked our careers the way Sugihara did.

But I remembered how I met Sugihara's wife in Israel. I asked her about her husband and what had motivated him to do what he did in defiance of the instructions of his own Government, at that point an ally of Nazi Germany.

She said people were standing under their windows. They wouldn't leave.

They stood day and night. Some, on their knees.

Sugihara saw their faces.

When the Soviet Union occupied sovereign Lithuania in 1940, thousands of Jewish/Polish refugees (who had already fled from Russian occupation of Eastern Poland) were desperate to get out of Lithuania. Consul Sugihara worked 18-20 hours a day, over the period of several weeks issuing transitory visas to Japan. By the time the Soviets ordered all diplomatic consulates closed, in late August 1940, Sugihara had saved about 2,300 lives. The story goes that he was still throwing blank visas with his signature out of the window of the train departing Kaunas. Even if that is nothing but a legend (as it is), I'm sure it is born out of admiration and gratitude of people whose lives Sugihara had saved. People for whom he was larger than life, a hero capable of unrealistic, legendary actions.

I met the descendants of these visa recipients, in Vancouver, Canada. I held in my hands the faded fragile pieces of paper with the stamp of a Japanese consulate and Sugihara's signature.

It's estimated that about 40,000 of these refugees' descendants are alive today.

Recently, I got from Denmark several messages from Yaroslav. He sent me a picture of a big loft that their host family gave them at their disposal. There were several pictures of the town they now lived in.

"We live in an incredibly beautiful city Esjberg right on the sea," Yaroslav wrote. "I like everything here. We were given a shelter by a couple in their early 30s. They treat us very well. They have two kids, a girl and a boy. The wife Agnes is very kind to us. Her husband Lucas helped us to fill out all the papers for the Government.

They also take care of all our expenses. For the Easter, they went to Norway and left the whole apartment at our disposal for 14 days. We met their neighbours who had also taken a Ukrainian mother with a child. Lucas and Agnes drove us around showing us different places in Denmark. I already made some friends. My mother also has connected with some people. She has calmed down though she is still home sick. We're very grateful for everything."

I will translate and send it to Mark, I told myself. I will.

10. Lettuce and Onions, Tomatoes and Watercress: Atanes and Basima

April 11, 2022 – (Korczowa, Poland) – June, 2022 (Vancouver, Canada)

FROM THE START OF HIS CAREER, President Zelensky, a heroic war time leader, both recognized the ethnic diversity of his country and called for its unity. A Jew whose mother tongue is Russian, addressing his compatriots and the world in Ukrainian and English, he appeals to the shared history and common cultural references of Ukrainians. He has every reason to call for unity. Historically, the fault lines between a predominantly Russian-speaking East, and an economically richer, European-oriented West divided the nation. A brutal aggression against all has now obliterated those divisions.

Ukrainian Greeks, Jews, Tatars, Roma, Armenians, Georgians are now one nation. Yet not all of them have equal rights once they escape the war.

An odd-looking couple these two were. Flabby, with a round, indifferent face of a withered sun-flower, the woman was twice the size of her scrawny, swarthy man who looked much older than her, in his late fifties. They looked lost as they wandered around the refugee centre, wheeling behind them their suitcases. While I talked to the man, the woman watched, scratching inside her whipped-up nest of a hair-do from time to time. Without saying a word, she turned around and went to look for a cot. Had the man been mute, his eyes alone would have spoken for him: deep brown velvet, framed with long thick lashes of a young girl, their whimsical dolefulness brought to my mind Bach's cello suites for some reason. He spoke in Russian with a strong Armenian accent, which signalled ... trouble. Clearly, Atanes knew that himself or at least anticipated, as he rambled something half-apologetically, his lower lip quivering.

Poland was full, they had to move on to some other European country, I intimated. But Atanes and his partner were not married, and that worried him. In the eyes of Europeans, as it turned out, that was the least of their problems.

The greatest one was their citizenship. The protection law adopted by the European Union applied to his Ukrainian partner, but not to him.

What might have mitigated the lack of a Ukrainian passport would be a permanent resident document issued to non-Ukrainian nationals living in Ukraine. But Atanes' had expired; he'd forgotten to renew it. Who could anticipate this war?

A free transportation to Armenia, the Armenian Embassy in Poland was ready to provide Atanes with, was hardly a solution in their situation: he had already made his life in Ukraine, to say nothing of his Ukrainian partner. And there was still another complication: an ethnic Armenian, Atanes was born in Nagorny Karabakh, officially belonging to Azerbaijan.

"I've already fled once," he said. "This is the second time."

In 1988, when the war in a disputed mountainous enclave, inhabited mostly by ethnic Armenians, broke out, Atanes was a young man. The struggle for independence from Azerbaijan brought over another war of 2020, and Atanes fled to Ukraine. Two years later, Russia attacked his new home: now he had to flee again with no place to go.

I went from one representative to another: Finland, Holland, Sweden, Denmark, Baltic States. All gave me the same answer: a refugee protection would be granted to Atanes' partner only.

The expression of Atanes' remarkable eyes had now changed. These were the eyes of a cornered animal: "The world is a hostile place; it will give me no mercy." I wondered for a moment if the memory of Armenian genocide continued to live in the genes of a nation, colouring Atanes' world view in such hopeless overtones. "Generational trauma," as psychologists call it.

"Israel? What about Israel?"

Israel was issuing visas to non-Jewish refugees fleeing the conflict. Under Israeli's Law of Return, they would not be eligible for immigration, but as long as the war lasted, they would get shelter, food, clothing, and basic health insurance.

"I would go, but she (Atanes referred to his partner), she wants to stay close to Ukraine. Somewhere in Europe."

I saw a piece of paper left on a counter top announcing new services for people in Atanes' situation. I copied the phone number: a voice on the other end advised to wait; a representative would arrive at the refugee centre that afternoon. I rushed to pass on the news of hope to Atanas and his partner, but ... they were nowhere to be found.

Short of a magic carpet transporting them to some enchanted land, with no wars, passport and border controls, where had they disappeared?

Would the world ever afford peace and home to Atanes, whose anguished soul spoke through his eyes more eloquently than any words?

* * *

Long tables pulled up together edge to edge, their zinc surfaces tightly covered with buns that lay open like clams: a lettuce leaf, a ring of tomato and cucumber, bits of onions, a slice of Swiss cheese on one side, mayo on the other; shut the flaps of a "clam"; wrap it in a cling wrap; arrange inside big crates in neat rows; cover with a lid, send over to several border crossings; start all over again. And again and again. I could never catch up with Basima, as her deft little hands cut, sliced and packed tirelessly, while she hummed something quietly under her breath. An ethnic Tatar married to a Russian, she and her husband both fled to Poland. Where would they go next? Who would welcome her husband, a man with a Russian passport, nowadays? Atanes' story repeating itself, I thought with alarm.

Yet, Basima and her husband Sergey came up with an ingenious solution. They now lived and volunteered at a refugee centre. Basima's domain was the kitchen.

Sergey, who knew some Polish, delivered food and did some work as a handyman.

Just like Atanes, Basima too was a refugee second time around.

In British Columbia, where I live, First Nations preserve an ancient belief: if a mother buries the umbilical cord of her child near home, the child will always return.

The first time the umbilical cord connecting Basima with her land was cut in 2014, when Russia annexed Crimea, Tatars' ancestral land since the 15th century. After the annexation, 60,000 residents of Crimea left for Ukraine. Half of these people were Crimean Tatars. This small ethnic group had good reason to escape. As soon as Putin took over Crimea, the Tatar Parliament (*Medzlis*) was abolished. The Tatar newspapers and television channels were forbidden, their homes searched, with arrests to follow. The Russian authorities prevented the Tatars from what was so important to them: honouring the memory of deportation victims.

* * *

Forced deportations of peoples, as a form of political repression, was practiced by the Soviet state since its conception. In Stalin's days, it grew in scope as to affect millions: Tatars, Jews, Moldavians, Western Ukrainians, Germans, Chechens, Ingush, Finns, Kalmiks were resettled thousands of kilometres away from their traditional homelands into remote and inhospitable lands with a low rate of survival. Others (usually ethnic Russians) were moved in to replace them.

Basima's grandparents were among 200,000 Crimean Tatars deported to Central Asia in 1944. The pretext? Stalin had accused the whole people of collaboration with the Nazis. (It's worth noting that, at the time of deportation, Crimea had already been freed from German occupation.) And does it not sound familiar today? Putin labelling Ukrainians "Nazis" and using it as a pretext for his unprovoked invasion?

In 1944, the "operation" of removing thousands of Crimean Tatars from Crimea was conducted with lightning speed. Thirty-two thousand NKVD (precursor of KGB) troops were dispatched. Several minutes to half an hour was allowed for packing. Those who resisted were shot down. Cattle cars moving people across the country stopped every now and then to throw cadavers out: children's bodies through the windows, adults' through the doors.

How many survived?

Nobody knows.

After the Soviet Union collapsed, the descendants of the deported began to repatriate to Crimea. At the same time, the Ukrainian Parliament recognized the deportation as a genocide and established a memorial day for its victims. The celebration of that day Putin tried to prevent when his 'green men' took over Crimea.

Basima was born in Crimea. She was seventeen when her family fled to Ukraine after Russians had annexed the peninsula.

Now, at twenty-eight, she was fleeing again.

I thought about it all, watching Basima joyfully humming some tune, as she moved along the table covered with 'clams.' A leaf of lettuce, a ring of tomato, a slice of Swiss cheese ...

I watched her, and thought how lucky I was to be alive; to have a place to return to.

I wouldn't be writing now had Stalin lived only a month longer than he did. The deportation of Jews to Siberia was planned for February of 1953.

Several hundred trains were already moved to Moscow railway stations and other cities.

I was just a toddler.

It's ironic that my grandfather was then a director, in charge of the major factory making trains. Did he know? And if he did, how did he, a Jew, feel living with this secret and not being able to do anything about it?

The cars were unheated, with room only for standing. Starvation and the organized attacks of local Robin Hoods, these "avengers of the Russian people" would make sure that only half of the deported would have reached their destination. The whereabouts of the barracks, labour camp style, built for the survivors, was a state secret. The then whispered rumours: the barracks had only three walls, to save construction material, a freezing death for the arrivals. Who could verify those rumours then and less so now?

In the meantime, massive preparations were under way: all over the vast country the lists were being created of "persons of Jewish nationality" (the word "Jew" had such a pejorative connotation as to be unprintable). The "operation" was planned in two stages. As a "purebred" I, together with my family, would have been deported first, and "half-breeds" later.

Stalin, a mass murderer with the theatrical imagination of a sadist, carefully orchestrated a preamble to that scenario.

The deportation itself was planned as a culmination of an earlier campaign over Jewish doctors accused of mass murders. Stalin planned a show trial of doctors for March 7, 1953, with the subsequent public executions for March 11-12. Shortly after the executions, thousand-strong meetings had to be held in major plants and factories with workers calling to punish the accomplices of Jewish murderers. Whipped up anti-Semitic hysteria would reach its apogee and turn into pogroms all over the country – a ripe moment for a publication of an open letter of well-known Jewish doctors condemning their murderous colleagues as the foes of human race. The letter would have contained the request to deport Jews to some far away place in order to protect them from the just wrath of the people. And then the circle would close: being a protector of Jews, Stalin will respond to the request.

As always, a theoretical justification of Stalin's actions from a Marxist perspective had to be provided. It was laid bare in the book "Why It Is Necessary to Deport Jews from the Industrial Centres of the USSR." The print run of one million copies was to be distributed all over the country. The reviews of the book were ready to be run on Central television and major newspapers. But somehow the well-oiled plan ran behind the schedule: disorganization, problems with the lists of deportees. On April 5, two days short of the show trials, an event of cosmic significance happened: Stalin suddenly died (or was poisoned, one theory says). And because of this, I am here, alive, writing this and still trying to connect the dots of my country-of-birth's tragic history.

Mayonnaise, lattice, watercress, a slice of tomato, cheese, and bacon for the destitute.

Let them eat, let them sate themselves.

And us, let us keep cutting. As long as we do, there will be hope for the world.

11. Maria of Korczowa

April 11, 2022 – (Korczowa)

A WOMAN ESCAPING WAR on her own was a rare sight in the stream of refugees crossing the border to Poland. Refugees usually came as families or neighbours. On rare occasions, common misfortune would unite total strangers.

But Maria travelled all alone.

I met her in a cafeteria, a busy place serving food at any time of day or night to both refugees and volunteers. But her table was free. She silently nodded when I asked if I could join her.

I glanced at her and – out of vague embarrassment – quickly looked away. In front of me was a woman of rare beauty.

A subdued glow emanated from her delicate, finely shaped face. I noticed how pale she was, her skin an alabaster hue. A perfect arch of her brows, a pure outline of her chin and lips, and those Botticelli eyes ...

Though sleeping areas of the centre were heated, chilly draughts danced through hallways and corridors.

Wrapped in several layers of clothing Maria visibly quivered from cold. Her long pale fingers curled around a cardboard mug she used more for warmth than for drinking. From time to time, she would tuck under her blue scarf long curls, the colour of ripe chestnuts. She sat in the corner, at the edge of her chair, still, but at the same time, slightly retreating, as if even the little space she occupied was too much for her. That elegant, sensuous line of her slender body, where had I seen it? She collected her scarf around her neck and in a flash I remembered: in front of me was Maria of Simone Martini's *Annunciation.* All I needed was to replace Maria's dark, taciturn, still Byzantine face of Martini with Botticelli's *Primavera.*

In her serene seclusion, Martini's Maria was reading The Scriptures (the way all Marias did) up to the very moment when the celestial apparition suddenly invaded her peace, blinding her with the radiant splendour of his wings. No, his Maria doesn't turn away from her fate handed over to her by a luminous messenger, the holder of an olive branch. She is depicted at a frontal angle, and we can clearly see her fear, her bewilderment; but her body instinctively shifts away from the intruder in one elegant swerve. With the timid gesture of her right hand, she gathers the edges of her dark blue robe around her neck, as if for protection.

Ave Gratia Plena!

You have been chosen.

Ave! You are the one, at fifteen.

Maria fled Dnipro, a city in the central-eastern Ukraine, after rockets had destroyed its airport and several apartment buildings.

"My grandparents were from Dnipro," I said. "I still have some relatives in Ukraine. But they are too old to evacuate."

"I see," Maria said dispassionately.

I visited Dnipro 3 years ago, looking for the street where my family used to live ... before they were executed with 25,000 other Jews, during WWII. I found the street, but nothing remained of their house.

"What's the name of the street?" Maria asked.

"Pushkin street."

"I know that street. One of my students lives there. I teach piano to children."

"Have you come here alone?"

She confirmed by a silent nod.

"Any family back home?"

"No ... not any more." Her lips parted allowing a quiet sigh to escape. "My husband died. He was older than me. Yes, recently. Of a heart attack."

In the silence that followed the din of voices became more pronounced. I hastened to change the subject.

"You teach piano to kids. Nice profession! You must be good at what you're doing ..."

"I don't know ... I just love children," she said quietly.

"Too bad I didn't have you as a teacher ..." I said, smiling. "I had bad luck as a kid: my teacher gave up on me pretty quick. Said I had no ear for music. The only thing I can play now is a dog's waltz."

I chuckled.

Maria shook her head, but didn't comment.

"That was still in the Soviet times. Either you were a Mozart or not worth spending any effort on. Actually, it's one of my biggest regrets in life ... I love music, you see."

"But musical talent can be developed! Not everybody is a Mozart!"

"Can you, as a teacher, tell, early on, if the child is talented or not?"

"Oh, sure."

"How? No child wants to practice scales, I assume."

"True, they all find scales boring. The difference is that a gifted child will be attracted to the piano. The child may not want to do your assignments, instead they want to explore on their own. They'll stray away, they'll experiment."

She quivered slightly.

"Are you cold?"

"A bit. I'm anemic, you see. Low hemoglobin."

"There is a medical centre here, in case you need something. What were we talking about? Oh, yes. Music. Long time ago, I had a friend. We were both students back then: she studied violin in Moscow Conservatory. I studied art history at the University. That was still Brezhnev's time."

"I was born when Ukraine was still part of the Soviet Union."

"Really? I would've never guessed. You look so young!"

"Oh, no! I'm 43. My daughter, 25. I was a kid when Ukraine became independent."

"Then you wouldn't know it, thank God ... for you, as a musician, that would have been terrible. See, students were dispatched to collective farms each September. Always a shortage of hands and the crops simply rotted. I actually didn't mind ... Better than Dialectical Materialism, Scientific Communism, all this nonsense we were stuffed with in the first year instead of art history, in my case. But my friend, a violinist, for her it was different. The living conditions in those farms were pretty awful. They had to scramble potatoes and beets out of mud with their bare hands all month long. No gloves to be had, of course, and in September it was usually cold and it rained. After a month of poking around in wet clay, violinists couldn't restore the flexibility in their fingers for the rest of the semester!"

Maria rubbed her fingers as if to make sure nothing went wrong with them. I sipped on my tea. Maria still didn't touch hers.

"I wanted to get some hot chocolate," she said. "They didn't have any today or yesterday. Maybe tomorrow."

"How long you've been here then?"

"Several days. Waiting for a flight to Spain. There is one tomorrow, they say."

"A flight? You have money for a ticket?"

"No, Wizz Air takes refugees for free. I get by train to Warsaw first. And then to the airport." Again she sighed.

"You have family in Spain or know somebody there?"

"Not really. I just like heat ... It's warm there, that's why."

I hesitated to tell her what I knew about Spain. The country had already accepted 130,000 Ukrainians. With all its good will, Spain had no means to accommodate that many. It came up with a scheme of absorbing the evacuated by stages. The first six months Ukrainians had to live in hostels in the cities chosen by social workers. They would eat all together in the canteens and get 50 euros a month, as all other needs (medical, educational) would be provided for. In the second stage, they would be placed in available families across the country. The third stage meant they would have to be independent and find a job. With an unforeseen and quickly growing inflation, many host families couldn't fulfill their obligations. With 15 per cent unemployment, even manual, low paying jobs, became scarce.

I spoke with caution:

"Spain had taken lots of refugees already. Without a language, professional jobs are almost impossible to find."

"My husband once went to Spain for a conference. He liked it there. He said to me ... how did he put it? Every stone in Alhambra sings, that's what he told me," Maria said dreamily.

For the first time I saw a shadow of smile on her face.

"Will you be looking for a job though?"

"Oh, yes, I'll have to work! When my husband was alive, we did quite well then. He was an architect and owned a company. He'd say, 'Masha, you work if you want to ... for pleasure. I'll take care of the rest.' My health was never great, you see ... and he didn't want me to get too tired ... But now ... now I have to work. I don't know languages, that's the problem. Just a bit of English."

I tried to think what jobs – realistically – could she find in some hypothetical country if she wanted to stay in her profession. Music teacher in a kindergarten? Not a bad idea, but without the language competing with the locals would be hard. On the other hand, isn't music itself a language? Hmm ... how about music as part of art therapy?

Ukrainian kids are traumatized and if, say, there could be found a way of bringing Ukrainian kids together or go to schools with many of them ... there was something in it, I felt.

"I don't know ... I've never really done anything like that," Maria said, fumbling the edges of her scarf. And again I sensed a slight shift in her body, an almost imperceptible withdrawal. Fighting for her place under the sun seemed to be too much for her. Planning ahead takes energy. She didn't have that, I could clearly see it.

We sat silently for a moment. She began to sip on her tea in tiny birdy gulps.

"You must know a lot of Ukrainian songs, I assume."

"Yes ... why?"

"I mean traditional songs, folklore. My grandmother used to sing to me when I was small. I just had an idea ... Everybody is interested in Ukraine right now. If you start performing folk songs, the audience will love it!"

"Oh, no, I am not a performer."

"Do you sing though? No? You can accompany amateur singers on the piano, then. I don't know about Spain, but in Canada there are church choirs, community choirs. They sing in different languages, different kinds of music. We have a large Ukrainian community in Canada. Second, third generation Ukrainians. Still nostalgic for the Old Country, for its songs, its music,"

"Old Country? Ukraine? That's funny!"

"That's what children of immigrants usually call countries in Europe their parents came from. Compared to North America, which is a New World for them. I remember singing along with my grandmother in Ukraine. I was just a child, and didn't understand the words, but the melody, the sorrow, it got to you somehow. One song especially I loved. How did it go?

> *"My beloved mother, you couldn't sleep a full night,*
> *Seeing me off at dawn, a long voyage lying ahead."*

"Forgot how it goes ... Can you sing along with me?"

Maria looked around with an obvious unease.

"Where are you staying? Why don't we go there?" I suggested.

Her cot was in the corner of a large area, between the wall and another cot whose occupiers were elsewhere at the moment. In the space in front, the kids were chasing each other, shouting, yelling. The heavy smell of unwashed bodies was overbearing.

"Please, sit down."

Maria sat at the corner, freeing for me the rest of her cot. She clasped her hands in her lap, closed her eyes and drew out in a small but pure soprano:

> *"My beloved mother, you couldn't sleep through the night,*
> *Seeing me off at dawn, a long voyage lying ahead."*

Her voice that had sounded flat and somewhat muted when she spoke, gained vibrancy with each note and was rising and falling in lamentation:

"Your tender mother's smile,
The embroidered rushnik[3] you gave me for good luck.
I'll take it and spread it out like my destiny."

I sang along, recalling some words, replacing others by humming: "*Over quiet rustling of grass and groves ...*"

"Take a touch higher here, on *grass and groves*. Like this," Maria said, encouraging me.

"See, I can't keep the pitch!"

"Oh, you're doing fine. You just need a little practice."

"And on that rushnik, everything painfully familiar will come to life:
Childhood, departure, and your mother's love.
Your tender mother's smile.
The embroidered rushnik you gave me for good luck,
I'll spread it like my destiny,
Your eternal loving smile. Your sad eyes."

Suddenly, as if Maria stumbled on something, her voice sagged and was extinguished, cut shot. Her eyes welled, she tried to blink away the tears, to control her voice, but it wobbled before drowning in frequent desperate sobs. I was lost for words, so unexpected this outburst of emotions was, so much at odds with her whole demeanour.

Instinctively I hugged her. She didn't resist and quickly pressed her wet face to my shoulder. That gesture, the feeling of her face next to mine, pierced me with a sharp

---

3 A towel.

93

sense of urgency. As if a clock began ticking inside me, each tick-tock stealing away the time that was left for me to act, to do something.

"He could have lived, my husband! But she killed him!" Maria kept repeating through the paroxysm of weeping.

"Who killed him, who, Maria?"

Through her crying, I finally figured out her story.

Maria's daughter had moved to Moscow several years before the war, working successfully in an advertising agency. When Putin attacked Ukraine, the daughter called her mother: "What's going on in Ukraine? Did you all go mad? Bombing your own hospitals, your own kindergartens? Couldn't you find a better way of settling scores with each other?"

In many phone calls that followed, Maria tried to get through her daughter's armour of misinformation. But that proved impossible. Words didn't mean anything any more. Ultimately, daughter stopped talking to her mother.

"Disturbed in her head, that's what she is," Maria said, knocking lightly on her temple.

I tried to comfort her. Most likely, her daughter knows the truth, but has to keep mum: a new law can send you to jail up to 15 years simply for using the word "war." A man was arrested in the street for carrying a sign: "War and Peace. Tolstoy."

"If it were just fear, I would've understood. But it's not that ... It's like ... like something happened to her brain! What I can't fathom is how my own daughter believes Putin more than she believes her parents? She calls us Nazis. I say to her, who is a Nazi? Am I a Nazi? Your father, a Nazi?"

For the first time I heard Maria raising her voice, colour coming to her face. "I told her who the real Nazis were: Russians! That's what we call them now:

Rushists: Russian Nazis!"

But Maria's husband wasn't to give up so easily. To replace cynical lies with facts, to make the voice of reason to be heard became his obsession. At one point, he called Moscow while the sirens were screaming in the background. "Stop pulling wool over my eyes, Dad," he heard his daughter's voice. "These are ambulances."

During the meal – the last one with his wife, as it turned out – he retold Maria his latest conversation with their daughter: "You set up those secret labs, with chemical weapon, you and your Americans! You are going to attack Moscow! The uncovered horrors in Bucha? They were staged by your actors, disguised as corpses with marks of torture painted."

After that phone conversation, father wobbled to the table. Maria tried to change the subject. But his glassy look scared her. For a while they ate in silence. Suddenly he choked. Then slid to the floor and half an hour later was dead from a fatal heart attack.

"Does your daughter know that you had to escape and are now in Poland?"

"Oh no. She doesn't care what happens to me, no ..."

Betrayal is like death, I thought. No court of law can rule against it.

But should she be left forever in a state of such despair?

"Maybe, just maybe," I said, "your husband had some undiagnosed heart condition before? It happens, you know ..."

I regretted I had said that. Maria gave me a tired, all knowing look: as far as she was concerned, her daughter's lies had killed her own father. Nothing would change her belief, that much was obvious.

3

Shortly before I met Maria, Canada had opened up for Ukrainian refugees. The government provided several free charter flights. None of them were flying to Vancouver where I lived, but I could arrange the ticket, I told Maria, should she consider going to Canada instead of Spain. I put my hand on top of Maria's: "I have an extra bedroom at my place. And a new puppy. Do come!"

"There's a large Ukrainian community in Vancouver. Two churches. One, with a big hall for social events, perfect for recitals. I think you sing beautifully, Maria, but if you just want to accompany on the piano, I'm sure we can find the singers. It'll be great success, you'll see! And then ... you know what? In Winnipeg and Edmonton there are large Ukrainians communities. We can try that too! It would be fun."

"But it cost money, all of that."

I told her not to worry. Canada has always welcomed immigrants. Syrian refugees, the most recent example. Several friends would join the efforts to sponsor a family and share the responsibilities; somebody would have a free basement or an extra room in the house; somebody would drive kids to school; somebody would try to find them jobs. What do you think?"

Maria lowed her head, her eyes extinguished.

"Look, if you decide to return to Ukraine, you can do that any time you wish," I quickly added.

"But ... but ... I have nothing to thank you with ..."

"You don't have to. All I want ... I just want to hear you play that song, about the embroidered *rushnik,* the one my grandmother used to sing. Oh, I'm kidding! I think you will be happy in Canada, you'll find some peace. And once you settle, you'll be able to live your own life, do whatever you love to do. I'm here for two more days. What do you think?"

"Let me think about it a little."

"You tell me tomorrow. I'll be here first thing in the morning."

4

Those Madonnas Maria resembled gave birth miraculously, without pain. More keen on immaculate conception, than on birth, the reliable sources don't specify how exactly the latter has happened. Most likely, during Virgin Mary's sleep, as a mystic dream of that rare sort that moulds into reality imperceptibly at your awakening. As soon as Virgin Mary dispelled the sweet nebula of her reverie, she discovered a baby at her side, that milky-white wonder, bathed in celestial light, with no traces of blood on his fair skin, a clean umbilical cord showing a bit, the awkward proof of the indelible link between His mother's humanity and His own divinity, pouring ever since into each other as through two communicating vessels. So that if the needy hoped for a divine intercession from the Son, they could as effectively pray to His Mother and be heard.

The Baby gave its first beatific smile to a Dove, alighted from above and enfolding with its white-snow wings the snapping of the umbilical cord and carrying it off for later much contested safeguarding in various reliquaries around the globe.

But Maria of the Korczowa refugee centre was too gentle for the brutal business of labour. She bit through her low lip trying – in vain – to subdue wild screaming: her nightgown was blood stained at the bottom as well as at the neck. The gates of her slender, small-boned 18 year-old-body couldn't open wide enough for two days; and for two days the sound of crackling resembled the cracking of a tree during the storm, before the trunk gives in and splits. When the surgeon finally slashed her with one stroke of his sabre, unleashing beastly high-pitch pain, her desire to die was finite.

The baby girl came into the world "in a shirt," that is, covered with an amniotic sack. According to strongly entrenched local beliefs, this rare happening promised a long, happy life to the baby; care-free walks of laughter along rivers of milk and honey.

Breastfeeding, Maria of Korczowa did not at all have the expression of serene tenderness, of a somnambulistic bliss the way Leonardo's Madonna Litta had, for example. This Maria cringed from pain, as her nipples, unaccustomed to the assault of the suckling gums, quickly broke into bleeding cracks, so that six times a day, the baby was consuming mother's milk mixed with blood. The only thing in common a careful observer would notice between Madonna Litta and Maria of Korczowa was the colour of their hair; shiny smoothness of ripe auburn chestnut, against the unblemished alabaster of their skin.

But soon the living Maria, tricked by nature, forgot all her troubles. She forgot it like every woman on earth does, less procreation stops. Her body forgot the pain, and sleepless nights, forgot the fatigue, and the discomfort that lingered for many months.

Spring came. The fleeting shadow of her daughter's first smile; the first attempts to hold upright the tender stalk of her head; the first time, those wide open, blue eyes held pensively the reflection of the cloudless sky, two azures merging. Now, holding the baby in her arms, Maria looked at her child exactly as all Marias of Old Masters did for centuries at theirs: with serene tenderness and all encompassing love.

The time came when the baby took its first unsteady steps on this benevolent earth. Maria brought her daughter to Dnieper, to the meadows dotted with white, blue and yellow flowers. She made a wreath of daises and cornflowers and put it on her daughter's reddish hair. Perhaps it was prickly, and the little one brushed it away crinkling her nose in a funny way that recalled her mother's. Then they both rolled in the grass laughing. And then Maria of Korczowa did something Madonnas of the Old Masters could not do: she began to teach her daughter piano. It turned out that the student had an easy, natural talent. The stage in a concert hall was looming. A little girl in a pink dress with a huge bow in her auburn hair, alone in front of a grand piano.

Down below, in the darkness, the ecstatic audience breaking into applause.

Yes, her daughter was born in a "shirt", after all.

5

A three-story building stood at the edge of the rural road running to the very border past wintry, black fields. With its empty halls, except for long tables moved to the centre and saddled over by chairs on all sides, the building looked like the semi-abandoned relics of the Soviet past, most likely used for Communist party and labour union meetings.

Under the very roof, at the end of a long corridor, several low-ceiling rooms were used as a cheap hotel, hostel style. There was no bathroom in my room, and no chairs. A bed, a chest of drawers, with a bedside table, accommodated my nights.

My eye tripped over dark stains of uncertain origin on the side of the mattress, which was wider than the rough sheet exposing them. The lukewarm radiators were no match for the penetrating cold moisture. I climbed into bed, pulled the clammy blanket over to my chin and listened to the soft sounds of rain against the skylight turning all of a sudden into a hard irregular buckshot. Hail has arrived. For some reason, I found its drumming soothing.

Before falling asleep, I emailed Laura, my closest friend, a psychiatrist.

—*I'm coming back with a Ukrainian refugee. She'll need a lot of help, psychological counselling. May I count on you?*

Laura had a flat in town and a cottage on one of the islands. Perhaps Maria could spend couple of days there? Three of us could go kayaking ...

— *What happened to her?* Laura responded right away.

Loss of a husband, home, livelihood. And on top of that, her daughter wouldn't speak to her mother. Brainwashed by Putin's propaganda, I wrote. *But Mother's heart is a forgiving heart. With time, when the war is over, I hope they'll reconcile. That Kazakh man won't forgive, but Maria ... Maria will.*

— *What Kazakh man?* Laura texted.

— *I met him two days earlier, by a sheer coincidence, at the same table where I met Maria in the morning. All dishevelled and scruffy, with a bowl of stew in front of him. Those sharp narrow eyes ... He looked oriental. Was of mixed parentage, he told me, his mother Ukrainian, his father, a Kazakh. As soon as he saw me (my badge of a volunteer singles me out), he pushed his bowl away and began to talk. An electrician by trade, from the Donbass area.*

— *How come he was allowed to leave Ukraine?*

— *Oh, he looked old enough. Definitely, more than 60. He found himself on the opposite sides of a barricade from his whole family. His son has been fighting on the Russian side ever since the Russians meddled in Donbass. His wife and daughter also whole-heatedly supported Putin's regime.*

— *Why did his son choose to fight against his own people?*

— *I asked him that very question. He just rubbed his thumb against his index and middle fingers: bubki, good dough, that's why! He had sold his soul to the devil. My whole family did. So I left and came here. Alone.*

6

The wind and the hail stopped. It was perfectly quiet now. Instead of helping me to fall sleep, that stillness brought my anguished thoughts into a sharper focus.

Putin may ultimately fail to win the war with Ukraine, but he had one victory assured: most Russians believed his propaganda and supported him and his war. Every war he waged only strengthened his power. Why? How did it happen? The majority of Russians, so called "deep people", "real" Russians of national roots and soil; the Russians of small villages and big industrial cities hailed every act of his aggression: Chechen, then Georgia, then the annexation of Crimea, and now, the whole of Ukraine.

—*It must be very late at your place? Why don't you get some sleep?* Laura texted across the ocean, thousands of miles away.

—*All right. I will. I just have to figure out one thing, Laura. Why does the land grab, the idea of attacking a free, sovereign nation appeal to Russians? And why the way the Russian army is going about it: ruthless bombing, raping, torturing, turning 14 million of their own neighbours into refugees, why, why does it leave Russians indifferent? Will a refrigerator ever win over a TV, as one writer, now an exile, has quipped? In other words, will a fridge, sooner or later emptied by sanctions, take an upper hand over propaganda? Or will the lack of goods only increase people's anger against the West, blaming it, as usual, for all their problems? What I wanted to say is that not 140 million Russians support him. Intelligentsia doesn't. Young people don't (or some don't, at least). But the majority doesn't really care, that's the problem. We know and we don't. We heard something, but we haven't. It's not up to us to decide – nothing depends on us. Cognitive dissidence, like in the Soviet times.*

— You need to take care of yourself. It seems to me that thinking about Putin and his war isn't very helpful, Laura cautioned me.

— Ok, Ok!

I shut down my laptop. But I couldn't shut down my mind.

What if ... what if the massive protests had happened at the very beginning of the war (now not possible), the way Solzhenitsyn imagined in one of his books (was it *Archipelago Gulag*?) What if, Solzhenitsyn asked, during the KGB arrests of Stalin's terror, while people were being pushed into the black cars, what if neighbours, witnesses had screamed? Not one person, but everybody? What if ...?

I suddenly got thirsty. I climbed out of bed and, without turning on the light, found a water bottle distributed for free in the refugee centre and took several gulps trying to calm down.

—Look, you're not a political scientist, nor a historian, a voice in my head was saying. You don't have the knowledge, the tools to analyze. Just go to sleep for Christ's sake! Tomorrow, another day in the refugee centre.

—True. I need to sleep, But I can't, the other voice was responding. I just need to figure one nagging god damn thing. What I need to know is this: why in the 21st century, Russians love their "Father Tzar"? just like they loved Stalin in the 20th?

—Wait, but why did the Germans love Hitler? The Chinese, their Mao? The French admired Napoleon, guilty of two million deaths? It's not in the realm of rational, is it? And besides, you can't stake a claim on understanding history! It's not your speciality!

—That's true! But all of a sudden, we're all in it, now, in this very moment, aren't we? All I want to understand is not the past, but NOW. This war. This refugee transit centre. These hundreds of women and children and old ailing men passing in front of my eyes day, after day, after day.

And Maria. She wouldn't have been here - if. (I am sure her husband died of a heart attack, no matter what I told her.) He wouldn't have died - if. Thousands upon thousands would not have been killed - if.

—So, the question remains: why, how, after all *Perestroyka* hopes, within three or four years, history took a U-turn, in the country of my birth? How did he win his compatriots' hearts?

—By the promise of economic prosperity that was meant only for himself and his cronies? No, you can't pull it off without big words. Nationalism, superiority of Russian soul; Russian exclusivity as a nation, combined with Russian resentment against the West, these were the logs he threw into a bonfire.

—But wait, Russian people are really talented people, will you argue with that?

—Of course not!

Russia has had first-rate scientists, writers, artists, athletes, musicians, four million of whom, by the way, have left or are leaving the country after he had started the war. But he doesn't care about the best in his nation. His ruse was some intangible *duchovnost*, "spirituality", an inherent understanding of higher spiritual values that lie above the rational, materialistic, corrupt West. Russia, as a Third Rome, as a torch bearer, a path blazer for the West lingering in the darkness. Yet the West is richer, freer, happier, technologically more advanced. After the fall of the iron curtain, the Russians could see it for themselves. How do you square that circle? By both using the West and resenting it, hating and envying it all in the same breath! That's the concoction the Tsar has offered his subjects. And they drank it. Willingly.

I'm shivering from cold but at the same time burning from inside. The cognitive dissonance I mentioned. The Stockholm syndrome. I know it first hand. I myself was its victim. How Maria cringed when I told her about my music teacher, who made me quit piano lessons in my childhood. Well, it wasn't her fault really. The reason she didn't want to teach me was because I had no time for her homework. Instead, I had 30-40 math problems to solve after each school day, my Stakhanovite norm. My math teacher, Zinaida Petrovna. I'll call her Z for short and what a strange appellation coincidence, not that every Russian tank boasts "Z" on its side.

Z had the dry body of a hound, thin, dead-looking hair collected in a tight knot at the back; acne on her flat, dour face, and a gritty male voice that instilled awe in her charges.

Her: punctual, collected, moving with relentless drive and covering a blackboard with formulas with such speed as if the school was about to catch fire.

Me: a slow, sloppy, absent-minded dreamer, with textbooks and copy books in perpetual disarray; losing pencils and pens and erasers and – disdainfully – ribbons from my braids. To sit in the class with your hair loose was an affront to Lenin's corner on the first floor; to the Council Squad on the second, to school in general, and to Z in particular.

How could Z not hate me?

Were my math abilities so poor? I'd say they were average, before Z took over my life, that is. On occasion, a premonition of harmony, a sense of wonder would alight on me when in grade three, a mysterious correlation between the sleek curve of parabolas and numbers would suddenly manifest itself.

Now looking back, I suspect that Z had very few pleasures in life. With her appearance and character, she couldn't have counted on the ordinary consolations of married life. She lived alone. I'm sure I provided her with some measure of robust fun when she called me up to the board in front of the class and I, in a foretaste of coming execution, would drop chalk to the floor, then glasses, searching for both in places they couldn't have fallen. Z's linguistic virtuosity would send the class into the paroxysm of laughter when she called out in her deep-throated rumble: "Just look at this halfwit, this nincompoop, this chicken brain, this wet rag! Why are you standing here like this? Who are you? Why am I wasting my precious time on you? Respond!"

I feel a strange sorrow for Z. I have ultimately outwitted and outnumbered her: I'm still alive and she, for sure, not. Unless with her formulas, she had cracked the secret of eternal life. I pity her with the same kind of pity I have for a Russian mother who has thanked Putin for giving her son the chance to die for the sacred cause of fighting fascism in Ukraine and defending Russia from the West.

But in those bygone days, I did live in perpetual fear of Z. And strange to recall, the more I feared her, the more I respected her. Knowledge is power, as Lenin said. Because of the chicken size of my brain, I could never match her in whipping up formulas on the blackboard. She had knowledge and I didn't. Yet, in spite of her wisdom, poor her had to suffer at my hands. How bored she must have been having to check hundreds of sums she insisted on assigning me. What an inconvenience I was in her life!

To make up for it, I once decided to give her flowers. I wanted her to know that even while she hated me, I respected, even loved her. At the end, I got cold feet: she could have taken my pure expression of love for a shameless bribe.

The term "Stockholm syndrome" had not yet been coined.

Would it have helped me had I known what dreaming of flowers for Z was called?

* * *

I woke up next morning with a sore throat and aching in every muscle. I stayed in bed the whole morning, but in the afternoon forced myself to get up and go to the refugee centre.

I was looking for Maria: paper work for Canada was extensive and there was no time to lose. She was not in the corner where we sat and sang together. A woman with two children was occupying her cot. I went to a cafeteria. To the medical post. I even checked the bathrooms.

I was about to dash to Spanish volunteers to check if Maria was on their list. But what was her last name? I had never asked.

Back home nothing has changed.

My usual, peaceful, serene days go by.

Where are you, Maria?

Walking the dog in the woods, I imagine you in Alhambra, in front of some colonnade, listening to the song of the stones, in the imaginary reunion with your husband; the reunion more important to you than any practical considerations.

12. The Journey to the Future, the Journey to the Past

October 1, 2022

SEVEN MONTHS HAVE PASSED since I left Poland. The war is escalating. Putin's so called "partial" mobilization will send to slaughter more than a million men, according to Ukrainian intelligence. As I'm writing this, men of all ages, professions and health conditions are being drafted indiscriminately, from the streets, walk-in clinics and subways stations. Fifteen per cent of Ukrainian territory is annexed as a result of a sham referendum. Tragically, the Ukrainians in occupied territories will be forced to fight against their own people. But not for long. Putin is losing his war. In case of a military defeat, most likely, he will lose his power.

Anti-mobilization protests were not significant; yet draft centres were being set on fire and hundreds of thousands young educated men fled the country.

Last week I got a note from Yaroslav telling me that his mother and he had returned from Denmark to

Ukraine. "Things didn't work out," was all I got by way of an explanation. This news has upset me. I thought about the Danish family that had welcomed them: and – selfishly – about my own efforts of persuading much troubled Oksana to go to Denmark, to look forward rather than backward and meet her new life with an open mind. All these efforts came to naught, it now seemed.

In the course of my life in Canada, circumstances forced me to change cities, houses, apartments. Like for many North Americans, home became a shifting and rather abstract concept: it's where work is; where ecology is good; where life is comfortable, where I can find new friends. Can I blame Oksana that her sense of home, her attachment to her land is different from mine? Perhaps not as warped? I can't pretend that in the two days of our encounters I had puzzled out her life. The limelight in the theatre illuminates one spot, leaving the rest in darkness. Kharkov region where they lived is now freed. But the Russians keep shelling the area. Will Oksana and Yaroslav be safe?

As if to soften my disappointment, Anastasia's letter came on the heels of Yaroslav's. Anastasia framed her feelings in quasi-religious terms: God was placing on their path the very best: the kindest and most generous people. Their hosts went out of their way to help them: bicycles were provided for the whole family; entertaining trips were organized and all their needs taken care of. Anastasia had already found a job; they were all learning Danish; teachers at school (both Danish and Ukrainian) were excellent. She was thanking me profusely and wished me God's eternal protection ... As I was struggling with tears, I must admit I couldn't remember who that balm-to-my-soul Anastasia was ... there were so many faces and voices. Until she sent me the pictures of herself and her three girls, basking in the sun somewhere on a beach, one with a flower wreath on her head, the two youngest chasing balloons. And then I remembered.

As my time at the Korczowa refugee transition camp was coming to an end, and the rest of the team had already left for Warsaw, I stayed for an extra day: I had promised those who were on a waiting list to get them on a bus to Denmark the next morning. A crowd of refugees surrounded me that last morning. It was chaotic. Anastasia, her husband and three daughters were in that crowd. I saw them just fleetingly.

Since the JDC team had already gone, I had to return to Warsaw on my own. I took off my badge, my bright blue vest, identifying me as a JDC volunteer, and joined the refugees waiting for a train to Warsaw. A small railway station with a cozy, domestic feel to it. Like everywhere on the refugee routes, free cookies, oranges and juices were neatly laid out on several tables covered with white clothes. Women with children quickly filled the train car to full capacity. There was more than a usual share of babies.

Ahead lay a six-hour journey from the border to the capital.

But an hour later, the sleepy quietness of the ride suddenly exploded: one baby screamed; others joined her, as by relay, and soon the whole car was in the throes of sobbing misery. It didn't last long though; mothers' efforts, combined with the rhythm of the wheels, soon restored peace. Dusk was falling. Behind the window pane, the still wintry landscape was running backwards; black fields with some wintry stubble, neat houses, leafless woods and groves were melting away. I was dozing off and through the haze of semi-consciousness the silhouettes of another scene came back to me.

It was 1995. Russia seemed to be on its way to democracy; the relationship with the West was friendly and several American agencies were busy helping Americans to adopt Russian orphans. Later, Putin would forbid the adoption by American citizens, but in 1995 nobody had yet heard of Putin.

On Christmas Eve, the Russian embassy in Washington decided to put on a special performance for American families and their recently adopted children. I flew to Washington D.C. to watch my son, an actor, in his role of Santa Claus. National flags of both counties, and huge Christmas tree sparkling with all kinds of baubles welcomed me in the hall of the embassy.

From my landing at the top of the stairs, I watched the ebb and flow of families down below: well-heeled, middle-aged couples; men in perfectly tailored suits that looked like successful businessmen, bankers, employees of the government; their wives in their best attire. From the top, I could see the neat partings of children's combed hair; their well-pressed little suits and festive dresses. Demurely, with an air of dignity, the elegant crowd took their seats in the amphitheatre-shaped hall.

Below, on a round stage, another huge Christmas tree was mounted. My son, a professional actor, dressed as

Santa Claus, was riding around the tree in a sleigh full of presents; his "granddaughter", Snow Girl, in an elaborate *kokoshnik* (traditional Russian head-wear), was singing and dancing, her dress all sparkles; the artificial snow was falling from above; the hanging stars were twinkling. And all of a sudden, the magic of a fairy tale was broken off by Baba Yaga, the Russian equivalent of a witch, who stormed onto the stage on her broom. As it should be, smoke and all kinds of scary noises accompanied her intrusion.

In fairy tales, Evil makes its appearance if only to foreshadow the final victory of Goodness. I don't think that the former orphans had been exposed in their Russian childhoods to many fairy tales to know this. Suddenly, an anguished howl pierced the air. It came simultaneously from several places, and spread like fire stripping away children's well-groomed masks. The newly-minted parents did their best to comfort and cajole their charges – to no avail. The decorum was broken and soon the whole hall was screaming, and the performance called off. All it took was a little scare for the children's old wounds to open up; for pain, anguish and deep-seated anxiety to burst through a thin veneer of genteel American life.

That's what I remembered while the train, full of refugees, was chugging along to Warsaw.

And inadvertently, I thought about what was happening now: of many thousands of Ukrainian children kidnapped and deported to Russia. I imagined the child centres the Russians are running (at least forty), some as far from Ukraine as Siberia and the Far East where children are brainwashed, their identity stolen: Ukrainian passports replaced by the Russian ones, any knowledge of Ukrainian history and culture substituted by Putin's propaganda. I imagined their confusion, their pain, their helplessness under the pressure of the Russian state. Recently Putin financed a program that would send these children to cadet schools in order to turn them into soldiers fighting their own Ukrainians.[4]

My painful thoughts were interrupted when I saw a tall, uniformed ticket collector stooping over me. I glanced at him and realized that I had forgotten to buy my ticket! What came next took me by surprise. We exchanged in reverse what would happen under normal circumstance: the ticket collector extended his hand to give me a ticket. I extended mine to receive it. Obviously, he took me for a refugee who could travel through Poland for free. I fit the picture: I had a backpack, was dressed like everybody else and, like everybody around me, I looked tired.

Perhaps he wasn't that far off. I was on a journey again; the journey that had started many years ago and still continued. I had been much younger then, and, in a way, foolhardy. Maybe this was because the future was so tightly sealed that it was pointless to try to second guess it; maybe it was because I had young children to think of; maybe it was because of a measure of fatalism that the Soviet experience instilled into everybody who

4   In March 2023, The International Criminal Court issued an arrest warrant for Putin over responsibility for war crimes including the deportation of 16,000 children. The Ukrainian government continues to document what they believe to be 110, 000 cases of deportation.

lived it. You knew you had no control over anything – your best strategy for survival was endurance and acceptance of things the way they came.

Though I spoke English and French, it helped me only partially. I didn't like the words "culture shock", yet I had no clue about so many things that any North American kid would have taken for granted: I didn't know there existed canned food for cats and dogs, and that a smiling cat's muzzle on a label didn't mean you could serve what's inside to your children, no matter how empty your wallet. The concept of private land was still vague to me: I didn't know that you were not supposed to walk through the fields any way you wanted because they belonged to somebody; that you couldn't sit on somebody's porch in the countryside even if your children were too tired to keep walking. I'd never seen white furniture before and thought that my first Ikea white desk was pure chic. And like refugees with whom I was now sharing this ride, I was grateful for the kindness of strangers. There was ambiguity in my gratitude. My pride suffered, as did theirs. I remembered now how those contradictory feelings had initially bothered me and how I tried to shuffle them under the carpet, for life would leave no time for soul searching.

But years later, when Russia opened up and I could finally visit my friends, the echoes of those early tribulations came back to me in an unexpected way. In one of my friends' apartment, I noticed my children's old book shelf. It was as rickety as it had been decades ago, with the same ink stains and scratches. Why did my friends keep such a useless thing all these years? But there it was, as if no time had passed; as if growing old was but an illusion; as if I hadn't lived several lives since then; hadn't visited many lands on several continents; hadn't tried my hand at so many different things. My past, my youth, were staring at me in my friends' semi-dark hallway.

"Do you remember," my friend said, "when you were leaving, we came over and you said: 'Please take whatever you need'?"

I didn't remember that, but yes, I may well have said it because in the '80s, hardly any possessions had been allowed through the border: I couldn't take my books with me; nor notebooks with my friends' phone numbers; the photographs of my grandfather, in a uniform, decorated with a row of medals for courage in the battles of WWII, were confiscated at the border. So yes, perhaps I did say that.

"Since then people have given me lots of things, especially at the beginning. To tell you the truth, it really bothered me."

My friend was surprised: "Bothered? Maybe because they were strangers? But we were happy to have your things! It was like part of you stayed with us. Your old keyboard, remember? Igor still uses it." She thought for a moment. "Isn't giving and taking the same thing? What we give to others will return to us? Under totally different circumstances, in a different shape, but it will. Things come full circle sometimes."

Passengers in the train car started to stir. Women were removing bags and suitcases from the shelves. The train was approaching Warsaw.

This amazing leg of my journey was coming to its end.

Afterword: Glory to Ukraine

AS THIS BOOK GOES TO PRESS, the war in Ukraine continues to rage. But more than ever, I'm convinced that Ukraine will prevail. What gives me such confidence? The Ukrainian army proved its ultimate courage, skill and ingenuity on the battle field. And the collective West (the US and Europe) moved from the reluctance to quarrel with Putin; from the fear of Putin's nuclear blackmail to a full understanding and resistance to his murderous intents. Very quickly Europe has successfully weaned itself from Russian oil and gas. And most importantly, the collective West pledged to support Ukraine militarily as long as it takes for Ukraine to win. Even though Putin has tried different strategies to break the spirit of Ukrainians, none of them worked. The infrastructure he aimed to destroy is being quickly restored; people have heat and electricity back in their homes and food in their stores that they manage to produce locally. In spite of the horrendous destruction ... of 14 million displaced ... of tens of thousand killed and wounded, the recent Ukrainian polls demonstrate that the overwhelming majority of Ukrainians would support peace negotiations only when the enemy de-occupy their country. In other words, the people are prepared to pay the ultimate price for their freedom and democracy.

That shows that the spirit of the nation is not broken. It's this spirit that will ultimately prevail over evil.

Ukraine, rebuilt and more united than ever, will enter the annals of history as the nation of heroes.

And what about Russia? It's destiny is tragic and my predictions are stark. Russia's present Neo-Nazi regime is bringing it to ruin: to economic, scientific and cultural isolation. The slightest dissent has been punished by life sentences. Duma (the Russian Parliament) is now discussing the introduction of capital punishment. Putin's propaganda has proved to be effective and has led to the moral corruption of the nation. His lies have turned millions into indifferent accomplices without any moral compass; thousands, into cynical sadists. In a notorious conversation intercepted by the Ukrainian intelligence, a young wife has instructed her husband to rape Ukrainian "broads" while using protection. Wives give their husbands a list of household items to be looted from Ukrainian homes; one said she needed a washing machine. A man on a subway was reported to the police by the informer who saw the image of the Ukrainian flag on that man's phone. The person was arrested and jailed. Mass weddings are shown on television: girls entice recently drafted men to marry them in order to get "coffin" money when they are killed. Often women hardly know their bridegrooms or have just met them. A mother bragged on TV that the "coffin" money bought her the make of a car that her perished son would have approved of. At the same time, the Russian government does all it can to avoid paying "coffin" money. Thousands of dead Russian soldiers remain in Ukrainian morgues, as Russia refuses to bring them home.

It will perhaps take several generations for the nation to come to its senses. But what will it take for Russia to be accepted again into the international community of peaceful democratic nations? I believe Russia will have to travel the same path as Germany did: it has to pay full reparations to Ukraine and to acknowledge its crimes; to cleanse itself inwardly from the terrible cancer by repenting publicly. It has to raise new generations of children who would know the truth about the history of their country, including the war with Ukraine and make sure it will never happen again.

And here we come full circle: the process of repentance can only begin when Putin is gone.

For that we all need Ukraine to win.

ACKNOWLEDGEMENTS

My gratitude to Włodzimierz Milewski for all he's done to support me through writing this book, as well as my previous ones. To him, also, belongs the concept and the early version of the book cover.

Thank you, too, to Michael Mirolla, and everybody in Guernica Editions, who saw the urgency of the subject matter and published the manuscript without any delay. I'm also indebted for careful reads of the manuscript to Brent Thomson, Ann Giardini, Eric Leif Davin, Claudia Casper, George Blumen, Alan Twigg and Robert Krell.

And finally, I am immensely grateful to many friends whose generosity showed Ukrainian refugees that Canadians take their plight to heart. My special thanks go to Tom Elliot, Cathy and Ian Aikenhead, Michael and Phyllis Moscovich, Doug Bolton, Donna Welstein and Bill Ehrcke, Elliana Tobias, Judy and Paul Meyer, Michael Barden, Barbara Buchanan, David Galloway, Thomas Kennedy, Barry Luger, Bill Kushlick, Della Ruth Swann, Victor Haines, and Daphne Gelbart.

About the Author

Marina Sonkina, a former lecturer in the Moscow State University and the CBC producer and broadcaster, teaches in the Liberal Arts Program at Simon Fraser University in Vancouver, Canada. She is the author of several books, including *Expulsion and Other Stories*, *Stalin's Baby Tooth*, and *Lucia's Eyes and Other Stories*. Her novel *Larissa* is scheduled for publication by Guernica Editions in 2025.